QUICK FACTS
ABOUT THE
U☆S☆A☆

by
NANCY HARTLEY

SCHOLASTIC INC.
New York Toronto London Auckland Sydney

ISBN 0-590-47403-0

12 11 10 9 8 7 6 5 4   5 6 7 8 9/9 0/0

Printed in the U.S.A.   40

First Scholastic printing, May 1995

This is a book dedicated to all "kids" who want to learn more about a country abundant in Freedom, enwrapped in Beauty, saturated with History, and still Hopeful. . . *America!*

— Nancy Hartley

WASHINGTON, DC

DISTRICT OF COLUMBIA
Became Capital of the United States in 1800

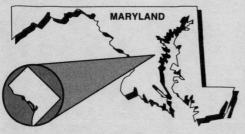

MARYLAND

★ **QUICK FACTS** ★

CAPITAL OF THE NATION

POPULATION: 598,790

AREA: 68.25 sq mi

NICKNAME: None

MOTTO: "Justice for All"

BIRD: Bald eagle, Wood thrush

TREE: Scarlet oak

FLOWER: American Beauty rose

Time Zone: Eastern, DST

HIGHEST POINT: 410 ft, Tenleytown in NW section

LOWEST POINT: Sea level, Potomac River

POSTAL ABBREVIATION: Washington, DC

GEOGRAPHY

Virginia is to its south and west, Maryland to its north, and Delaware to its east.

4

HISTORY

The Piscataway Indians were first to
live in this region. Later settlers founded
Alexandria in the colony of Virginia.
Congress decided to locate the capital along
the Potomac River, and George Washington
chose the place. In 1791, he chose land west of the
Potomac, including lands from Maryland and Virginia.
Pierre-Charles L'Enfant, a French architect and engineer,
planned this city, making the Capitol the center, with the
Mall extending from the Capitol. It was named by
Congress in honor of George Washington.

WASHINGTON, DC

SPORTS AND RECREATION

A good walking city with many museums, national treasures, historical offerings, parks, and cultural events. Washington's spectator sports include football's Washington Redskins, who play at R.F.K. Stadium, Washington Bullets basketball, and Washington Capitals hockey.

ATTRACTIONS OF INTEREST

☞ John F. Kennedy Memorial Center

☞ Vietnam Veterans Memorial

☞ National Zoological Park

☞ Lincoln Memorial

☞ Martin Luther King, Jr., Memorial Library

☞ Smithsonian Institution

☞ Washington Monument

☞ United States Capitol

☞ White House

WASHINGTON, DC

ECONOMY

- ⇨ Federal government
- ⇨ Research and development firms
- ⇨ Tourism
- ⇨ Publishing
- ⇨ Education

1ST FAMOUS FIRSTS

First in tourism
First in number of federal
  government positions
First in cultural activities
  (plays, operas, theater)

FAMOUS PEOPLE

Washington, DC, is the heart of our country's government. Famous people from all walks of life live and work there. The most famous is the current President of the United States.

FURTHER INFORMATION

D.C. Chamber of Commerce
1301 Pennsylvania Avenue
Suite #309
Washington, D.C. 20004

ALABAMA

**22nd State,
December 14, 1819**

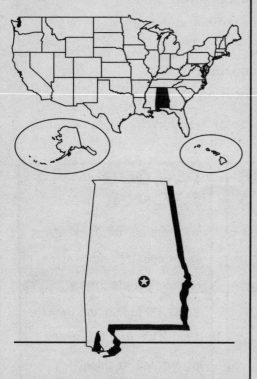

★ QUICK FACTS ★

CAPITAL: Montgomery

POPULATION: 4,089,232

AREA: 51,705 sq mi,
ranks 29th

NICKNAME: Yellowhammer
State

MOTTO: "We Dare Defend
Our Rights"

BIRD: Yellowhammer

TREE: Southern pine

FLOWER: Camellia

SONG: "Alabama"

TIME ZONE: Central, DST

HIGHEST POINT: 2,407 ft,
Cheaha Mountain

LOWEST POINT: Sea level,
Gulf of Mexico

POSTAL ABBREVIATION: AL

GEOGRAPHY

The state terrain is diversified with coastal plains
including prairie black belt and hills. Located in the
southeastern United States, Alabama extends north
to south from Tennessee to the Gulf of Mexico. It is
east of the Mississippi River.

HISTORY

The name Alabama comes from the
Choctaw, meaning "thicket clearer" or
"vegetation gatherers." Longtime inhabitants
of this land were the Cherokee, Chickasaw,
Choctaw, and Creek Indians. The French,
British, and Spanish struggled for control throughout the
seventeenth and eighteenth centuries. In 1702, the French
established the first settlement in Mobile Bay. The English
ruled after the French and Indian War. Montgomery,
where the Confederate States of America was formed,
became the capital in 1846. In 1870, Alabama produced
iron, creating a great iron and steel center. In 1915, the
boll weevil devastated the cotton crop. In 1933, the
Tennessee Valley Authority built a system for flood control.

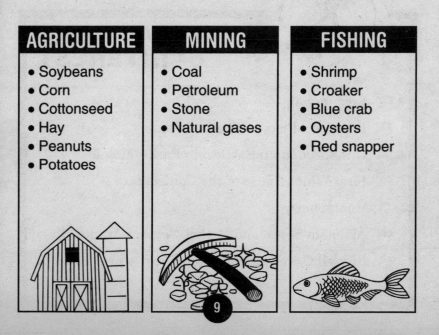

AGRICULTURE

- Soybeans
- Corn
- Cottonseed
- Hay
- Peanuts
- Potatoes

MINING

- Coal
- Petroleum
- Stone
- Natural gases

FISHING

- Shrimp
- Croaker
- Blue crab
- Oysters
- Red snapper

ALABAMA

SPORTS AND RECREATION

Miles of beaches attract water sports as does the
Tennessee River, with its lakes. Skiing is available in
Cloudmont in the northeast corner of the state.
Several resorts are also available in the state
parks. Spectator sports include football
played by the University of Alabama's
Crimson Tide and Auburn
University's Tigers.

ATTRACTIONS OF INTEREST

☞ Birmingham Zoo

☞ Discovery Place—Birmingham

☞ U.S.S. *Alabama* Battleship Park—Mobile

☞ First White House of the Confederacy—
Montgomery

☞ Alabama Space and Rocket Center—Huntsville

☞ Russell Cave National Monument—Bridgeport

10

ECONOMY

- ⇨ Pulp
- ⇨ Paper
- ⇨ Chemicals
- ⇨ Electronics
- ⇨ Apparel
- ⇨ Lumber

- ⇨ Food processing
- ⇨ Metals
- ⇨ Cast iron
- ⇨ Plastic pipe
- ⇨ Mobile homes
- ⇨ Poultry processing

1ST

FAMOUS FIRSTS

First satellite into space—
Redstone Arsenal
First blast furnace—
Pittsburgh of the South
(produced pig iron)
First Confederate capital—
Montgomery, Feb. 8 to May
21, 1861. Jefferson Davis
was inaugurated here.
First permanent settlement—
Fort Louis

FAMOUS PEOPLE

Hank Aaron

Tallulah Bankhead

Paul "Bear" Bryant

George Washington Carver

Nat "King" Cole

FURTHER INFORMATION

Alabama Business Council
State Chamber of Commerce
468 S. Perry ST
P.O. Box 76
Montgomery, AL 36195

ALASKA

**49th State,
January 3, 1959**

GEOGRAPHY

Alaska is located in the northwest corner of North America. It is bordered on the east by Canada, on the north by the Arctic Ocean, and on the south by the Pacific Ocean. To its west is Russia.

HISTORY

The name Alaska comes from the Aleut
Indians and means "great land" or
"mainland." In 1741, Vitus Bering and Alexi
Chirikov discovered Alaska and the Aleutian
Islands for Russia. The United States bought it from
Russia in 1867. It was called "Seward's Folly" because it
cost two cents an acre. In 1896, there was a gold rush.
First settled by Native Alaskans, Alaska became a U.S.
territory in 1912.

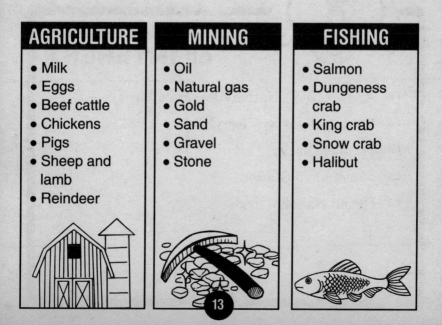

AGRICULTURE	MINING	FISHING
• Milk	• Oil	• Salmon
• Eggs	• Natural gas	• Dungeness crab
• Beef cattle	• Gold	• King crab
• Chickens	• Sand	• Snow crab
• Pigs	• Gravel	• Halibut
• Sheep and lamb	• Stone	
• Reindeer		

ALASKA

SPORTS AND RECREATION

Winter sports, helicopter rides to the glaciers, train rides, a ferryliner that serves coastal areas, festivals, and sled-dog races all attract visitors to this state.

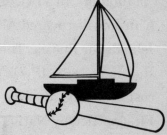

ATTRACTIONS OF INTEREST

☞ Arctic Coast—Native Alaskan village

☞ Marine Highway—ferryliner

☞ Portage Glacier

☞ Mendenhall Glacier

☞ Denali National Park

ECONOMY

- Oil
- Gas
- Tourism
- Commercial fishing
- Furs
- Lumber and wood products
- Native craftwork
- Printing and publishing

FAMOUS FIRSTS

First in value of fish caught by commercial fishermen

First settlement by Russians—Kodiak Island, 1784

First in gas and oil fields in size in North America—the Pridhoe Bay

First new state to join the union since Arizona and New Mexico in 1912

FAMOUS PEOPLE

Tom Bodett

Susan Butcher

Jefferson "Soapy" Smith

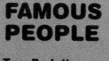

FURTHER INFORMATION

Tourist Information
Alaska Division of Tourism
P.O. Box 110801
Juneau, AK 99811–0801

ARIZONA

**48th State,
February 14, 1912**

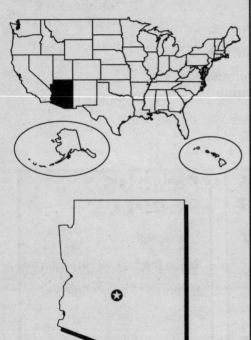

★ QUICK FACTS ★

CAPITAL: Phoenix

POPULATION: 3,749,693

AREA: 114,000 sq mi, ranks 6th

NICKNAME: Grand Canyon State

MOTTO: "God Enriches"

BIRD: Cactus wren

TREE: Paloverde

FLOWER: Blossom of saguaro cactus

SONG: "Arizona March Song"

TIME ZONE: Mountain, DST on Navajo Reservations only

HIGHEST POINT: 12,670 ft, Humphreys Peak

LOWEST POINT: 100 ft, Colorado River

POSTAL ABBREVIATION: AZ

GEOGRAPHY

Arizona is a southwestern state. Mexico is to its south, Colorado and New Mexico to its east, Utah to its north, and Nevada and California to its west.

HISTORY

The name Arizona comes from an
Indian word, *Arirzonac*, meaning "small
spring." In 1821, Spain ceded Arizona to
Mexico. After the Mexican War in 1848, the
United States took this territory. The Apache Wars
continued until Geronimo surrendered in 1886.

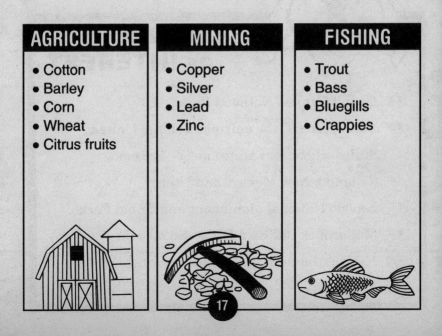

AGRICULTURE	MINING	FISHING
• Cotton	• Copper	• Trout
• Barley	• Silver	• Bass
• Corn	• Lead	• Bluegills
• Wheat	• Zinc	• Crappies
• Citrus fruits		

ARIZONA

SPORTS AND RECREATION

Arizona's climate offers many outdoor activities including rodeos, state fairs, golf, tennis, horseback riding, bicycling, hiking, and camping.

ATTRACTIONS OF INTEREST

☞ Grand Canyon National Park

☞ Four Corners (the only point in the United States where four states meet—Arizona, Colorado, New Mexico, and Utah)

☞ Navajo National Monument and Tribal Park

☞ McCormick Railroad Park—Scottsdale

☞ Native American ceremonial celebrations

ECONOMY

- ⇨ Manufacturing
- ⇨ Tourism
- ⇨ Mining
- ⇨ Arts and crafts
- ⇨ Agriculture

1ST FAMOUS FIRSTS

First continuously inhabited settlement in United States—Oraibi, built by Hopi Indians

First college built on an Indian reservation—Many Farms, Navajo Community College, 1969

FAMOUS PEOPLE

Cochise

Geronimo

Barry Goldwater

Zane Grey

Carl Hayden

FURTHER INFORMATION

Arizona Office of Tourism
1100 W. Washington
Phoenix, AZ 85007

ARKANSAS

25th State,
June 15, 1831

GEOGRAPHY

Located in the southwestern central United States, Arkansas has five main land regions. The Arkansas Valley divides two highland regions—the Ozark Plateau and the Ouachita Mountains. The Mississippi Alluvial Plains and the West Gulf Coast form its lowlands. The Mississippi River forms its eastern border. The Arkansas River flows southeast across Arkansas.

HISTORY

The name Arkansas comes from the native word meaning "downstream people." Arkansas first belonged to France, then Spain, and then France again. Arkansas fought on the Confederate side during the Civil War. The only diamond mine in North America is located in this state. William Jefferson Clinton, the 42nd President of the United States, was once governor of Arkansas.

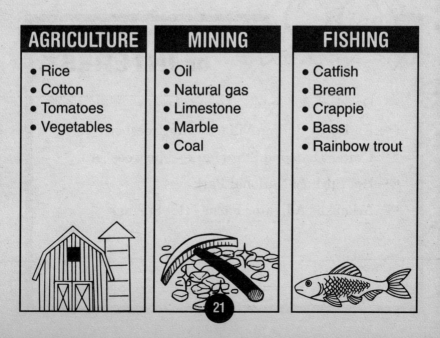

AGRICULTURE

- Rice
- Cotton
- Tomatoes
- Vegetables

MINING

- Oil
- Natural gas
- Limestone
- Marble
- Coal

FISHING

- Catfish
- Bream
- Crappie
- Bass
- Rainbow trout

ARKANSAS

SPORTS AND RECREATION

Due to Arkansas's vast number of lakes and 9,000 miles of streams, water sports are plentiful. Duck hunting is popular in the fall. Other sports are Mammoth Spring rafting and trout fishing.

ATTRACTIONS OF INTEREST

- ☞ Ozark Folk Center—Mountainview
- ☞ Ka-Do-Ha Indian Village—Murfreesboro
- ☞ Crater Diamond State Park—Murfreesboro
- ☞ Hot Springs National Park
- ☞ Arkansas Alligator Farm—Hot Springs

ECONOMY

- Food products
- Chemicals
- Lumber
- Home appliances
- Paper
- Motors
- Furniture
- Airplane parts
- Apparel
- Machinery
- Petroleum products
- Forestry
- Aviation and aerospace products
- Tires
- Shoes

1ST

FAMOUS FIRSTS

First permanent white settlement, 1686

First diamond field in America—Murfreesboro, 1906 (John Huddlestom found the first diamond)

First oil well drilled—El Dorado field, 1921

FAMOUS PEOPLE

Johnny Cash

Glen Campbell

William Jefferson Clinton

James W. Fulbright

Douglas MacArthur

FURTHER INFORMATION

Chamber of Commerce
One Spring Bldg.
Little Rock, AR 72201-2486

CALIFORNIA

**31st State,
September 9, 1850**

★ QUICK FACTS ★

CAPITAL: Sacramento

POPULATION: 30,379,872

AREA: 158,706 sq mi, ranks 3rd

NICKNAME: Golden State

MOTTO: "Eureka" (I have found it)

BIRD: California valley quail

TREE: California redwood

FLOWER: Golden poppy

SONG: "I Love You, California"

TIME ZONE: Pacific, DST

HIGHEST POINT: 14,494 ft, Mt. Whitney

LOWEST POINT: 282 ft, Death Valley

POSTAL ABBREVIATION: CA

GEOGRAPHY

California is located on North America's western coast, with the Pacific Ocean to its west. Northeast are the Sierra Nevada mountains. South is Mexico; on its northern border is Oregon.

HISTORY

California was named by the Spanish after a treasure island in a Spanish tale. Miners, the "forty-niners," were attracted to this land for its goldfields and brilliant sunshine, thus giving it the nickname the Golden State. First settled in San Diego by the Spanish in 1769, California became a U.S. territory in 1847 when the Mexicans surrendered it to John Fremont. The California Gold Rush began in 1848 when James Marshall discovered gold at Sutter's Mill, beginning a migration to California.

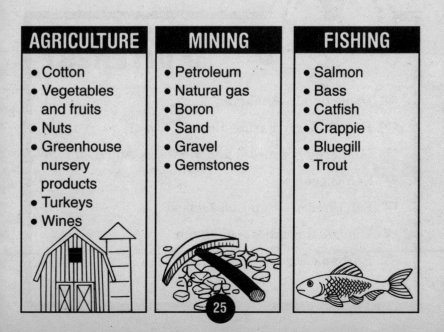

AGRICULTURE

- Cotton
- Vegetables and fruits
- Nuts
- Greenhouse nursery products
- Turkeys
- Wines

MINING

- Petroleum
- Natural gas
- Boron
- Sand
- Gravel
- Gemstones

FISHING

- Salmon
- Bass
- Catfish
- Crappie
- Bluegill
- Trout

CALIFORNIA

SPORTS AND RECREATION

Beaches, resorts, and ski areas offer outdoor activities of every kind. The cities of Los Angeles, San Francisco, and San Diego support professional teams in baseball and football. Theme parks, such as Disneyland and Universal Studios, can be found up and down the state.

ATTRACTIONS OF INTEREST

- ☞ Disneyland—Anaheim
- ☞ Knott's Berry Farm—Buena Park
- ☞ Monterey Peninsula and Monterey Aquarium
- ☞ San Diego Zoo
- ☞ San Simeon—San Luis Obispo
- ☞ Universal Studios—Anaheim
- ☞ Burbank Studios—Burbank

ECONOMY

- ⇨ Manufacturing: transportation equipment, metals, electronic equipment, biotechnology, missiles, communications for aerospace, computers, and TV equipment
- ⇨ Agriculture
- ⇨ Tourism
- ⇨ Entertainment

1ST FAMOUS FIRSTS

First in dairy production
First major earthquake—1906
First commercial film—*The Count of Monte Cristo*, Los Angeles, 1907
First discovery of gold—1848

FAMOUS PEOPLE

William R. Hearst

Jack London

Richard M. Nixon

Sally Ride

John Steinbeck

FURTHER INFORMATION

Chamber of Commerce
1201 K ST
Sacramento, CA 95814

COLORADO

38th State,
August 1, 1876

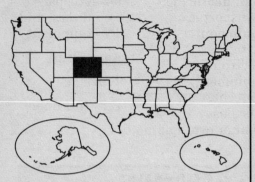

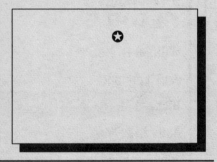

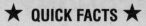 **★ QUICK FACTS ★**

CAPITAL: Denver

POPULATION: 3,476,000

AREA: 103,730 sq mi, ranks 8th

NICKNAME: Centennial State

MOTTO: "Nothing Without Providence"

BIRD: Lark bunting

TREE: Colorado blue spruce

FLOWER: Rocky Mountain columbine

SONG: "Where the Columbines Grow"

TIME ZONE: Mountain, DST

HIGHEST POINT: 14,433 ft, Mt. Elbert

LOWEST POINT: 3,350 ft, Arkansas River

POSTAL ABBREVIATION: CO

GEOGRAPHY

Colorado is located in the western central United States. Utah is on its west. Running north to south are the Rocky Mountains. Its eastern neighbors are Kansas, Nebraska, and North and South Dakota.

28

HISTORY

The name Colorado comes from the Spanish word for "ruddy" or "red." In 1806, Colonel Zebulon Pike explored the mountains north and west, finding the mountain that now bears his name, Pikes Peak. Most of Colorado became part of the United States with the Louisiana Purchase of 1803. In 1858, gold was discovered in Denver. The discovery of major silver lodes in Georgetown followed. The mining towns became wealthy. In 1876, Colorado became a state, one hundred years after the signing of the Declaration of Independence, thus giving it its nickname, the Centennial State.

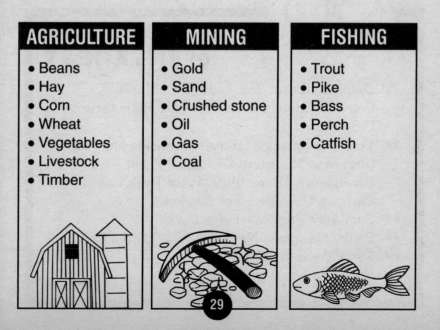

AGRICULTURE
- Beans
- Hay
- Corn
- Wheat
- Vegetables
- Livestock
- Timber

MINING
- Gold
- Sand
- Crushed stone
- Oil
- Gas
- Coal

FISHING
- Trout
- Pike
- Bass
- Perch
- Catfish

COLORADO

SPORTS AND RECREATION

With Colorado's vast mountain ranges offering recreational areas with lakes and resorts, outdoor activities are abundant throughout the year. Rodeos, skiing, water sports, hiking, camping, horseback riding, mountain climbing, and tennis are also popular.

Spectator sports include football (Denver Broncos and University of Colorado Buffaloes) and basketball (Denver Nuggets).

ATTRACTIONS OF INTEREST

☞ Denver: Denver Zoo, Children's Museum, Colorado History Museum, Gate Planetarium, U.S. Mint

☞ Colorado Springs: Lakeside Amusement Park, Cheyenne Mountain Zoological Park, Broadmop's Alpine Slide, Pikes Peak Cog Railway, U.S. Air Force Academy

☞ Sombrero Stables—Estes Park

☞ Rocky Mountain National Park—Estes Park

☞ Mesa Verde National Park

ECONOMY

- ⇨ Tourism
- ⇨ Aerospace
- ⇨ Government (military bases and an Air Force academy)
- ⇨ Electronics equipment

- ⇨ Agriculture
- ⇨ Manufacturing: computer equipment, aerospace products, and machinery

FAMOUS FIRSTS

First discovery of silver— Tabor Leadville, 1878

FAMOUS PEOPLE

Molly Brown

Jack Dempsey

Douglas Fairbanks

Scott Hamilton

Lowell Thomas

Byron R. White

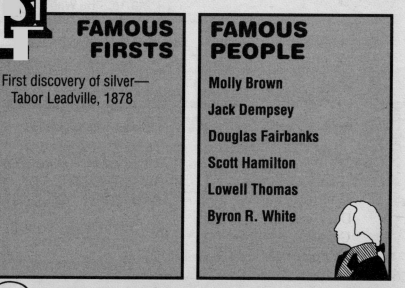

FURTHER INFORMATION

To learn more, call 1-800-433-2656 or contact the Chamber of Commerce in the city or town you plan to visit.

CONNECTICUT

**5th State,
January 9, 1788**

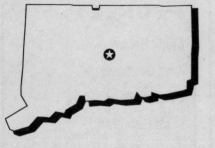

GEOGRAPHY

Connecticut borders three states: Rhode Island to its east, Massachusetts to its north, and New York to its west. New England's longest river is the Connecticut River, which bisects the state. It flows 407 miles. Along its southern border lies Long Island Sound, with 250 miles of shoreline.

CONNECTICUT

HISTORY

Between 6,000 and 7,000 Indians lived along the Quinnentugut, or "long tidal river," later named the Connecticut River. The Pequots, Algonkians, and Mohegans were the Indian tribes. In 1636, Reverend Thomas Hooker founded Hartford, on the site of a former Dutch trading post. From 1703 to 1875, New Haven and Hartford were each the state capital. More than 30,000 men of Connecticut joined the Continental Army during the Revolution. Half of George Washington's troops in 1776 were from Connecticut. Between 1768 and 1800, during the Industrial Revolution, paper mills appeared in Norwich.

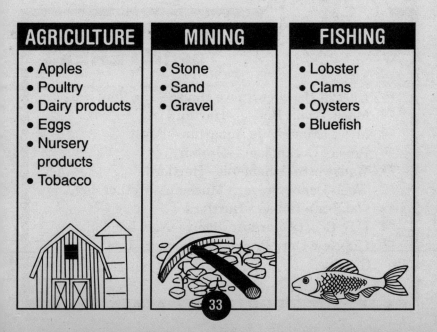

AGRICULTURE

- Apples
- Poultry
- Dairy products
- Eggs
- Nursery products
- Tobacco

MINING

- Stone
- Sand
- Gravel

FISHING

- Lobster
- Clams
- Oysters
- Bluefish

CONNECTICUT

SPORTS AND RECREATION

In addition to boating, fishing, golfing, hunting, skiing, and other outdoor activities, Connecticut is home to the Hartford Whalers hockey team.

ATTRACTIONS OF INTEREST

- ☞ Harriet Beecher Stowe House—Hartford
- ☞ Mark Twain House—Hartford
- ☞ Mystic Marinelife Aquarium—Mystic
- ☞ Project Oceanology—Groton
- ☞ Wadsworth Atheneum—Hartford
- ☞ Webb-Deane Stevens Museum—Wethersfield
- ☞ Old State House—Hartford
- ☞ U.S. Coast Guard Academy—New London
- ☞ Old New Gate Prison and Copper Mine—East Granby

ECONOMY

- ➪ Military (submarine base)
- ➪ Manufacturing: aircraft engines and helicopters
- ➪ Chemical production
- ➪ Insurance companies

1ST

FAMOUS FIRSTS

First submarine—The *Turtle*, 1776

First law school—The Litchfield School, 1784

First nuclear-powered submarine—U.S.S. *Nautilus*

First in manufacturing—Eli Whitney, in 1798, produced guns made by machines

FAMOUS PEOPLE

Ethan Allen

Samuel Colt

Thomas Gallaudet

Charles Goodyear

Katharine Hepburn

J. Pierpont Morgan

Harriet Beecher Stowe

Eli Whitney

FURTHER INFORMATION

State of Connecticut
Department of Environmental Protection
State Office Building
165 Capitol AVE
Hartford, CT 06106

DELAWARE

**1st State,
December 7, 1787**

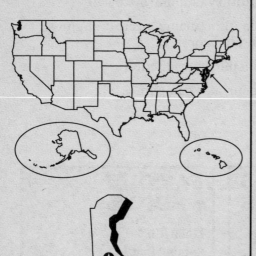

GEOGRAPHY

Located on the Atlantic coastline, it shares the Delmarva Peninsula with parts of Virginia and Maryland. Pennsylvania is to its northwest.

HISTORY

The name Delaware comes from
Delaware Bay and River, which were
named for Thomas West, Lord De La Warr.
Delaware was discovered by Henry Hudson
for the Dutch in 1609. It was settled then by the
Swedish in 1638, in Wilmington, and called New Sweden.
The Dutch forces took over, led by New Netherlands
Governor Peter Stuyvesant, in 1655. The English settled
here in 1664. Delaware fought in the American Revolution
as an independent state. It became the first state to ratify
the Constitution in 1787. Even though Delaware had
slavery, it did not secede from the Union during the Civil
War.

AGRICULTURE	MINING	FISHING
• Broiler chickens • Corn • Soybeans • Milk • Broccoli	• Sand • Gravel • Magnesium	• Crabs • Clams • Deep-sea fishing of tuna and marlin

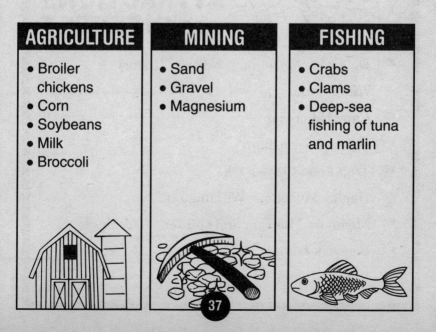

DELAWARE

SPORTS AND RECREATION

Delaware has miles of coastline, many lakes, ponds, attractive resorts, amusements, and water sports. Clamming and crabbing are especially popular. Many museums add cultural interests.

ATTRACTIONS OF INTEREST

☞ Delaware Museum of Natural History—Wilmington

☞ Cape Henlopen

☞ Delaware seashore

☞ Trap Pond State Park

☞ Hagley Museum—Wilmington

☞ Memours Mansion and Garden—Wilmington

☞ Fenwick Island

☞ Rehoboth Beach

ECONOMY

⇨ Manufacturing: food products, chemicals, elastic, and rubber

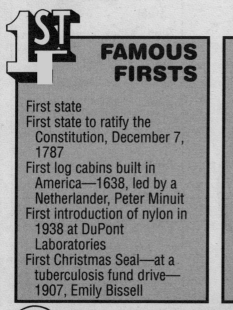

FAMOUS FIRSTS

First state

First state to ratify the Constitution, December 7, 1787

First log cabins built in America—1638, led by a Netherlander, Peter Minuit

First introduction of nylon in 1938 at DuPont Laboratories

First Christmas Seal—at a tuberculosis fund drive—1907, Emily Bissell

FAMOUS PEOPLE

Thomas Bayard

Henry Seidel Canby

E. I. DuPont

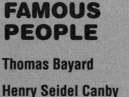

FURTHER INFORMATION

Chamber of Commerce
One Commerce Center
Wilmington, DE 19801

FLORIDA

**27th State,
March 3, 1845**

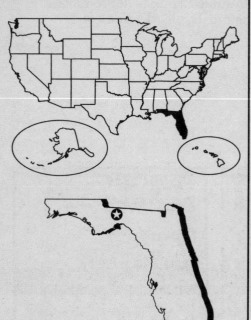

GEOGRAPHY

Florida is a low-lying peninsula at the southernmost
tip of the eastern United States.

HISTORY

The name Florida comes from the Spanish word meaning "Feast of Flowers Easter." The explorer Juan Ponce de Leon named it when he discovered the area on Pasqua Florida, "Flowery Easter," or Easter Sunday, 1513. He claimed Florida for Spain. Spain, England, then the United States would own Florida at different times. Many wars were fought with the Seminole Indians, ending in 1842.

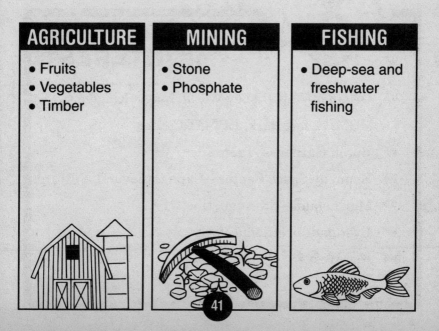

AGRICULTURE	MINING	FISHING
• Fruits • Vegetables • Timber	• Stone • Phosphate	• Deep-sea and freshwater fishing

FLORIDA

SPORTS AND RECREATION

Florida attracts people all year round due to its beautiful warm weather. Water sports are popular, as are all outdoor activities. Spectator sports include college and professional teams, including the Miami Dolphins and Tampa Bay Buccaneers of the NFL and Miami Heat of the NBA. The arts are available in theater, music, and dance as well.

ATTRACTIONS OF INTEREST

☞ Orlando: Walt Disney World, Magic Kingdom, MGM Theme Park, EPCOT Center

☞ Busch Gardens—Tampa

☞ Kennedy Space Center—Cape Canaveral

☞ Marineland—St. Augustine

☞ Everglades National Park

☞ Key West

ECONOMY

- ➪ Tourism
- ➪ Transportation equipment
- ➪ Printing and publishing
- ➪ Agriculture

1ST

FAMOUS FIRSTS

First city in United States—
St. Augustine, 1565

First U.S.-launched manned
spaceship—Cape Canaveral,
1961

First spacecraft to land on
moon—Apollo 11, from
Cape Kennedy, July 16,
1969

FAMOUS PEOPLE

Chris Evert

Henry Flagler

James Weldon Johnson

Joseph Stilwell

Charles Summerall

FURTHER INFORMATION

Florida Division of Tourism
126 Van Buren ST
Tallahassee, FL 32399–2000

GEORGIA

**4th State,
January 2, 1788**

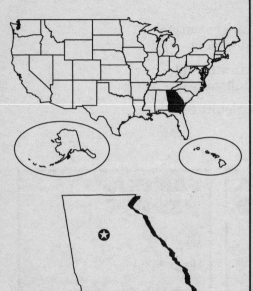

GEOGRAPHY

Georgia is a southern Atlantic state, with Florida to its south, North Carolina and Tennessee to its north, and South Carolina to its east.

HISTORY

Georgia was first explored by Hernando de Soto in 1540. General James Oglethorpe established a safe settlement in Georgia for people from England who owed money. Named in honor of George II of England, Georgia is known as the Peach or Goober State because of its large production of peaches and peanuts. During the Civil War Atlanta was burned to the ground by General William Tecumseh Sherman, leader of the Union army. The Civil War began and ended in Savannah.

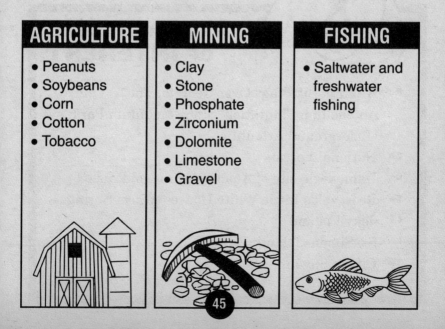

AGRICULTURE

- Peanuts
- Soybeans
- Corn
- Cotton
- Tobacco

MINING

- Clay
- Stone
- Phosphate
- Zirconium
- Dolomite
- Limestone
- Gravel

FISHING

- Saltwater and freshwater fishing

GEORGIA

SPORTS AND RECREATION

Spectator sports include baseball's Atlanta Braves, the Atlanta Falcons of the NFL, the Atlanta Hawks of the NBA, and college sports. Georgia's mild climate offers outdoor recreation from water sports to biking, hiking, tennis, golf, and more. The arts are represented as well.

ATTRACTIONS OF INTEREST

☞ Atlanta: Six Flags Over Georgia, The Antebellum Plantation, Stone Mountain Park, Underground Atlanta

☞ National Forests

☞ Dahlonega, site of America's first gold rush

☞ Roosevelt's Little White House—Warm Springs

☞ Jekyll Island

☞ St. Simons Island

☞ City of Savannah

ECONOMY

- ⇨ Tourism
- ⇨ Forestry
- ⇨ Agriculture
- ⇨ Textiles
- ⇨ Food
- ⇨ Apparel

- ⇨ Electronic machinery
- ⇨ Chemicals
- ⇨ Transportation equipment
- ⇨ Lumber

FAMOUS FIRSTS

First gold rush in America—Dahlonega, 1828

First Coca Cola served—Atlanta, 1887

First Girl Scout troop—Savannah, 1912, Juliette Gordon Low

First cotton gin—Savannah, 1793

First steamship to cross the Atlantic—S.S. *Savannah*, Savannah to Liverpool, England, 1819

FAMOUS PEOPLE

Griffin Bell

James Earl Carter

Ray Charles

Ty Cobb

Martin Luther King, Jr.

James Oglethorpe

Jackie Robinson

FURTHER INFORMATION

Chamber of Commerce
235 International BLVD
Atlanta, GA 30303

HAWAII

**50th State,
August 21, 1959**

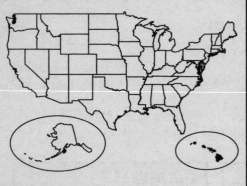

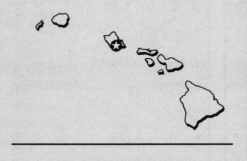

★ **QUICK FACTS** ★

CAPITAL: Honolulu (on the island of Oahu)

POPULATION: 1,134,750

AREA: 6,471 sq mi, ranks 47th

NICKNAME: Aloha State

MOTTO: "The Life of the Land Is Perpetuated in Righteousness"

BIRD: Nene (Hawaiian goose)

TREE: Kukui

FLOWER: Yellow hibiscus

SONG: "Hawaii Ponoi"

TIME ZONE: Pacific

HIGHEST POINT: 13,796 ft, Mauna Kea

LOWEST POINT: Sea level

POSTAL ABBREVIATION: HI

GEOGRAPHY

The only state that does not lie on the mainland of North America, Hawaii is located in the northern Pacific, 2,397 miles southwest of San Francisco, California.

HAWAII

HISTORY

Hawaii may have been named by
Hawaii Loa, the island discoverer. Its
nickname, Aloha State, comes from the
Polynesians' friendliness to tourists. Among
other things, aloha means "love" in Hawaiian.
Polynesians first sailed to Hawaii from other Pacific
islands in the year A.D. 300. In 1778, British Captain
James Cook named the islands the Sandwich Islands.
Queen Liliuokalani was replaced by Sanford Dole as
President of the Republic of Hawaii in 1894. In 1900,
Hawaii became a U.S. territory. Japan attacked Pearl
Harbor, a naval base, on December 7, 1941, bringing the
United States into World War II.

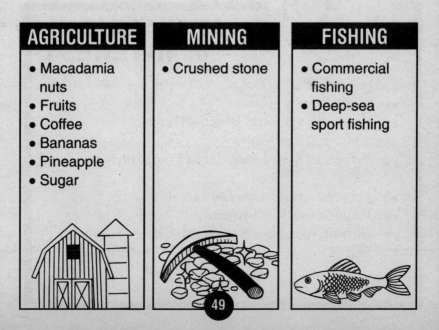

AGRICULTURE

- Macadamia nuts
- Fruits
- Coffee
- Bananas
- Pineapple
- Sugar

MINING

- Crushed stone

FISHING

- Commercial fishing
- Deep-sea sport fishing

HAWAII

SPORTS AND RECREATION

Since Hawaii's chief industry is tourism and its weather is so beautiful, many people take advantage of water sports, rodeos, hula festivals, biking, hiking, horseback riding, helicopter tours, and all other outdoor activities. The Hula Bowl college all-star football game is a favorite.

ATTRACTIONS OF INTEREST

- ☞ Sea Life Park—Oahu
- ☞ Aloha Tower—Oahu
- ☞ Kaimu Black Sand Beach—Hawaii
- ☞ Iolani Palace—Oahu
- ☞ U.S.S. *Arizona* Memorial at Pearl Harbor—Oahu
- ☞ Polynesian Cultural Center—Oahu
- ☞ Waimea Canyon—Kauai
- ☞ Hawaii Volcanoes National Park

ECONOMY

- ⇨ Tourism
- ⇨ Defense
- ⇨ Sugar
- ⇨ Pineapple
- ⇨ Government
- ⇨ Agriculture

- ⇨ Movies
- ⇨ Fishing
- ⇨ Manufacturing: sugar foods and canned pineapple

1ST

FAMOUS FIRSTS

First time islands were united—King Kamehameha, 1795

First U.S. President to visit Hawaii—Franklin D. Roosevelt, 1934

First vote for a President of the United States by Hawaiians—1960

FAMOUS PEOPLE

Bernice Pauahi Bishop

John A. Burns

Daniel K. Inouye

Queen Ka'ahumanu

King Kamehameha the Great

Queen Liliuokalani

FURTHER INFORMATION

Chamber of Commerce
Dillingham Bldg.
735 Bishop ST
Honolulu, HI 96813

IDAHO

**43rd State,
July 3, 1890**

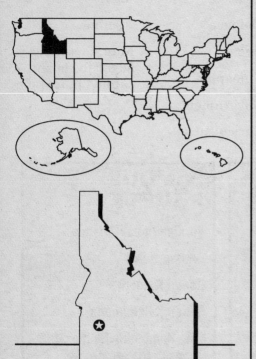

★ QUICK FACTS ★

CAPITAL: Boise

POPULATION: 1,039,295

AREA: 83,564 sq mi, ranks 11th

NICKNAME: Gem State, Spud State, Panhandle State

MOTTO: "It Is Perpetual"

BIRD: Mountain bluebird

TREE: White pine

FLOWER: Syringa

SONG: "Here We Have Idaho"

TIME ZONE: Mountain/Pacific, DST

HIGHEST POINT: 12,662 ft, Borah Peak

LOWEST POINT: 710 ft, Snake River

POSTAL ABBREVIATION: ID

GEOGRAPHY

Located in the northwest, Idaho is a mountain state. British Columbia is to its north, Nevada and Utah to its south, Montana and Wyoming to its east, and Oregon and Washington to its west.

HISTORY

Idaho is called the Gem State because it is a leader in the production of minerals, especially silver. The United States acquired Idaho as part of the Louisiana Purchase of 1803. The first to settle here were the Mormons in 1860. In the 1860's, miners, farmers, and cowboys came here to strike it rich with gold. The miners later left, but the farmers and cowboys stayed and worked this rich, fertile land and built a state.

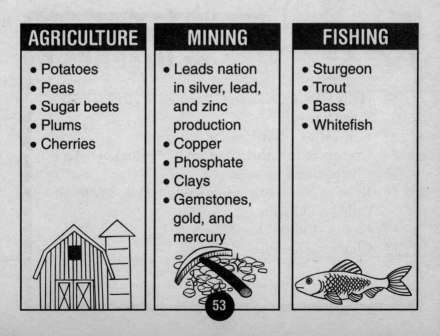

AGRICULTURE

- Potatoes
- Peas
- Sugar beets
- Plums
- Cherries

MINING

- Leads nation in silver, lead, and zinc production
- Copper
- Phosphate
- Clays
- Gemstones, gold, and mercury

FISHING

- Sturgeon
- Trout
- Bass
- Whitefish

IDAHO

SPORTS AND RECREATION

Winter and summer sports are popular in Sun Valley, Coeur d'Alene, Salmon River, and other areas. Water sports are available at many streams and lakes. Biking, hiking, and camping are available in national forest parks. The Snake River Birds of Prey Natural Area near Boise offers the opportunity to see falcons, eagles, ospreys, owls, and hawks. The nation's largest elk herds attract hunters.

ATTRACTIONS OF INTEREST

- ☞ Hells Canyon National Recreation Area—Snake River Canyon
- ☞ Sun Valley—Sawtooth Mountains
- ☞ Craters of the Moon National Monument—Arco
- ☞ City of Boise
- ☞ River of No Return (Salmon River) at Sawtooth Valley and Basin
- ☞ Caves—Crystal Ice, Shoshone Ice
- ☞ Ghost towns—Silver City

ECONOMY

⇨ Agriculture

⇨ Tourism

⇨ Mining

⇨ Electronics

⇨ Manufacturing: processed foods, chemical products, wood products, and lumber

FAMOUS FIRSTS

First in silver production
First in lead and zinc
First electricity from atomic
   energy turned on at a lab
   near Idaho Falls, 1951

FAMOUS PEOPLE

William Borah

Frank Church

Fred Dubois

Chief Joseph

Sacagawea

FURTHER INFORMATION

Department of Commerce
700 W. State ST
Boise, ID 83720

ILLINOIS

**21st State,
December 3, 1818**

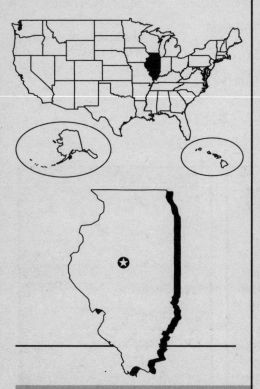

★ QUICK FACTS ★

CAPITAL: Springfield

POPULATION: 11,622,000

AREA: 56,345 sq mi, ranks 24th

NICKNAME: Prairie State

MOTTO: "State Sovereignty, National Union"

BIRD: Cardinal

TREE: White oak

FLOWER: Native violet

SONG: "Illinois"

TIME ZONE: Central, DST

HIGHEST POINT: 1,235 ft, Charles Mound

LOWEST POINT: 279 ft, Mississippi River

POSTAL ABBREVIATION: IL

GEOGRAPHY

A midwestern state, Illinois is bordered on its west, south, and east by the Mississippi, Wabash, and Ohio Rivers.

ILLINOIS

HISTORY

The name Illinois comes from an Indian word and French suffix meaning "tribe of superior men." The French explorers Jacques Marquette and Louis Joliet were first here in 1673. By 1763, the British won this land after the French and Indian War. With the opening of the Erie Canal, and the Black Hawk War ending the Indian conflict, there was heavy migration. Illinois became pro-Union in 1861, led by a U.S. Senate contender who lost, Abraham Lincoln.

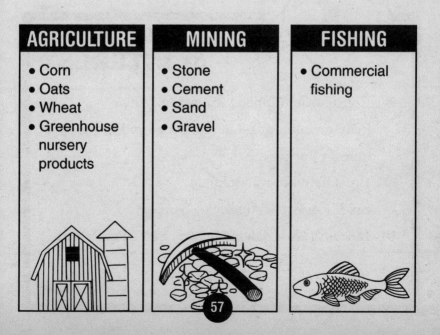

AGRICULTURE

- Corn
- Oats
- Wheat
- Greenhouse nursery products

MINING

- Stone
- Cement
- Sand
- Gravel

FISHING

- Commercial fishing

SPORTS AND RECREATION

Lake Michigan offers the opportunity to enjoy windsailing and sailing. Hiking and camping are popular, along with a variety of winter sports. Spectator sports include Chicago Bears football, Chicago Bulls basketball, Chicago White Sox baseball, and Chicago Black Hawks hockey.

ATTRACTIONS OF INTEREST

☞ Chicago: John Shedd Aquarium, Adler Planetarium, Museum of Science and Industry, Lincoln Park

☞ Brookfield Zoo—Brookfield

☞ Six Flags Great America—Gurnee

☞ Lincoln's New Salem Historic Site—Petersburg

ECONOMY

⇨ Agriculture

⇨ Hogs

⇨ Manufacturing: railroad cars, clothing, furniture, tractors, liquor, and watches

FAMOUS FIRSTS

First steel plow—Grand Detour, 1837, John Deere
First railroad sleeping car, The Pullman—Bloomington, 1859, George Pullman

FAMOUS PEOPLE

Jane Addams

Saul Bellow

Jack Benny

Ray Bradbury

John Deere

Abraham Lincoln

Ronald Reagan

Carl Sandburg

Frank Lloyd Wright

FURTHER INFORMATION

Illinois Dept. of Commerce and Community Affairs
620 East Adams ST
Springfield, IL 62701

INDIANA

**19th State,
December 11, 1816**

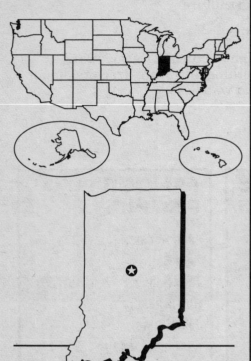

★ **QUICK FACTS** ★

CAPITAL: Indianapolis

POPULATION: 5,609,616

AREA: 36,185 sq mi, ranks 38th

NICKNAME: Hoosier State

MOTTO: "The Crossroads of America"

BIRD: Cardinal

TREE: Tulip tree

FLOWER: Peony

SONG: "On the Banks of the Wabash, Far Away"

TIME ZONE: Eastern/Central; counties near Louisville, Cincinnati, EDT; counties near Chicago and Evansville, CDT

HIGHEST POINT: 1,257 ft, Bethel

LOWEST POINT: 320 ft, Ohio River

POSTAL ABBREVIATION: IN

GEOGRAPHY

A midwestern state, Indiana's northern border is Lake Michigan.

HISTORY

The name Indiana comes from the native name meaning "land of the Indians." The Mound Builders had settled here also. The French and British fought over this land, with a British victory in 1763. During the Revolutionary War the Americans fought and won this land. Frequent Indian uprisings occurred here, finally ending in 1811 at William Henry Harrison's victory at Tippecanoe. Indiana remained a cultural force in the Midwest and prospered through the Civil War. It is one of the nation's leading manufacturing states.

AGRICULTURE	MINING	FISHING
• Corn	• Crushed stone	• Pike
• Soybeans	• Cement	• Walleye
• Wheat		• Catfish
• Oats		• Bass
• Rye		
• Tomatoes		
• Onions		
• Livestock		

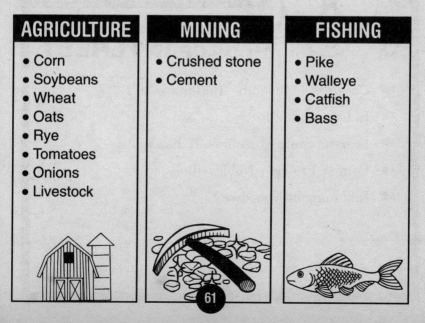

INDIANA

SPORTS AND RECREATION

The numerous lakes attract water sports at the many resorts. Biking and walking tours are popular. Winter sports, including skiing and sledding, are available throughout Indiana. Spectator sports include the Indianapolis Speedway.

ATTRACTIONS OF INTEREST

☞ Children's Museum—Indianapolis

☞ Indianapolis Zoo

☞ Indiana State Museum—Indianapolis

☞ Conner Prairie—Noblesville

☞ Indianapolis Speedway

ECONOMY

⇨ Agriculture: corn

⇨ Manufacturing: iron, steel, auto parts, aircraft engines, recreation vehicles, pharmaceuticals, and wood products

FAMOUS FIRSTS

First rapid-fire gun, a machine gun firing 250 shots a minute—1862

FAMOUS PEOPLE

Larry Bird

James Dean

David Letterman

Jane Pauley

Cole Porter

Dan Quayle

Red Skelton

Wilbur Wright

FURTHER INFORMATION

Chamber of Commerce
1 N. Capitol, Suite 200
Indianapolis, IN 46204

IOWA

**29th State,
December 26, 1846**

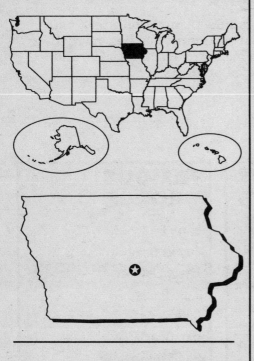

★ QUICK FACTS ★

CAPITAL: Des Moines

POPULATION: 2,795,220

AREA: 56,290 sq mi, ranks 25th

NICKNAME: Hawkeye State

MOTTO: "Our Liberties We Prize and Our Rights We Will Maintain"

BIRD: Eastern goldfinch

TREE: Oak

FLOWER: Wild rose

SONG: "Song of Iowa"

TIME ZONE: Central, DST

HIGHEST POINT: 1,670 ft, Osceola County

LOWEST POINT: 180 ft, Mississippi River

POSTAL ABBREVIATION: IA

GEOGRAPHY

A midwestern state, Iowa is bordered on the west by the Missouri River and on the east by the Mississippi River.

IOWA

HISTORY

The name Iowa comes from the native name, "this is the place," or "the beautiful land." Prehistoric Indians called Mound Builders first inhabited Iowa. After they disappeared, settlers found 10,000 burial mounds with tools and weapons. The land was heavily inhabited by Indians, including the Sioux, Miami, Iowa, Omaha, Oto, and Sauk and Fox, who were forced out by the French. The nickname Hawkeye State honors Black Hawk, a famous Indian chief of the Sauk and Fox. Iowa became part of the United States with the Louisiana Purchase in 1803.

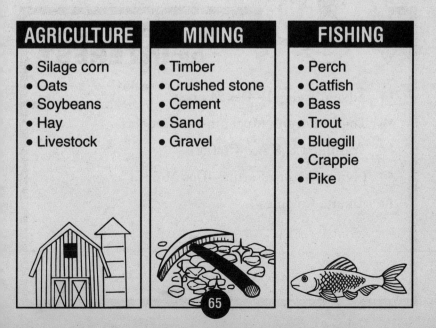

AGRICULTURE

- Silage corn
- Oats
- Soybeans
- Hay
- Livestock

MINING

- Timber
- Crushed stone
- Cement
- Sand
- Gravel

FISHING

- Perch
- Catfish
- Bass
- Trout
- Bluegill
- Crappie
- Pike

IOWA

SPORTS AND RECREATION

The Mississippi, Missouri, Des Moines, and Iowa Rivers attract water sports. There are also lakes in the northern part of Iowa with equal popularity for all water sports. Winter sports—skiing, skating, and snowmobiling—are popular in these areas as well.

ATTRACTIONS OF INTEREST

☞ Adventureland—Des Moines

☞ The Children's Museum—Bettendorf

☞ Trainland U.S.A.—Colfax

☞ Living History Farms—Des Moines

☞ Amana Colonies

ECONOMY

⇨ Agriculture: farmlands rank second only to California in livestock and crops.

⇨ Insurance companies

⇨ Manufacturing: non-electrical machinery and electrical equipment

⇨ Printing and publishing

⇨ Fabricated products

FAMOUS FIRSTS

The first state in the nation to study child development—Iowa City, 1917

First U.S. commercial educational TV station—WOI-TV, Iowa State University in Ames, 1950

FAMOUS PEOPLE

Mamie Dowd Eisenhower

Herbert Hoover

Glenn Miller

John Wayne

Meredith Wilson

FURTHER INFORMATION

Division of Tourism
Iowa Dept. of Economic Development
200 E. Grand AVE
Des Moines, IA 50309

KANSAS

**34th State,
January 29, 1861**

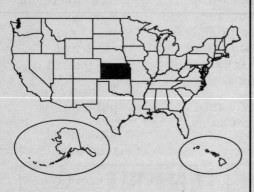

★ QUICK FACTS ★

CAPITAL: Topeka

POPULATION: 2,498,000

AREA: 81,823 sq mi, ranks 13th

NICKNAME: Sunflower State

MOTTO: "To the Stars Through Difficulties"

BIRD: Western meadowlark

TREE: Cottonwood

FLOWER: Native sunflower

SONG: "Home on the Range"

TIME ZONE: Central/Mountain, DST

HIGHEST POINT: 4,039 ft, Mt. Sunflower

LOWEST POINT: 680 ft, Verdigris River

POSTAL ABBREVIATION: KS

GEOGRAPHY

A midwestern state, its eastern border is the Mississippi River.

HISTORY

The name Kansas comes from a Sioux Indian word meaning "people of the South Wind." The Spanish explorer Francisco Vásquez de Coronado first explored Kansas in 1541. Kansas became a U.S. territory as part of the Louisiana Purchase in 1803. Forts Leavenworth, Scott, and Riley were established in the early to mid-1800's to protect travelers along the Santa Fe and Oregon Trails. Kansas earned the name "Bleeding Kansas" because of intense conflicts between pro- and antislavery forces before the Civil War.

AGRICULTURE

- Wheat
- Corn
- Oats
- Barley
- Soybeans
- Livestock

MINING

- Oil
- Natural gas
- Natural gas liquids
- Stone
- Salt

FISHING

- Lake and river recreational fishing

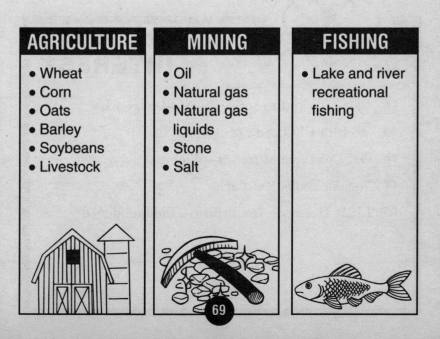

KANSAS

SPORTS AND RECREATION

Water sports are popular at the many reservoirs, state parks, lakes, and recreation areas. Canal trails are mapped out throughout the state.

ATTRACTIONS OF INTEREST

☞ Boot Hill and Frontier Town—Dodge City

☞ Wichita Children's Museum

☞ Old Cowtown Museum—Wichita

☞ Topeka Zoological Park

☞ Little House on the Prairie—Independence

ECONOMY

- ▷ Agriculture
- ▷ Mining
- ▷ Aerospace
- ▷ Machinery
- ▷ Manufacturing: aircraft, processed foods, petroleum products, and farm machinery

FAMOUS FIRSTS

First helium discovered at Dexter—1903

First state to plant Turkey Red, a new winter wheat variety—1870's

First Pony Express station to remain unchanged—Hanover

FAMOUS PEOPLE

Amelia Earhart

Dwight D. Eisenhower

Wild Bill (James Butler) Hickok

FURTHER INFORMATION

Kansas Dept. of Commerce
Travel and Tourism Division
400 S.W. 8th ST, 5th Floor
Topeka, KS 66603

KENTUCKY

**15th State,
June 1, 1792**

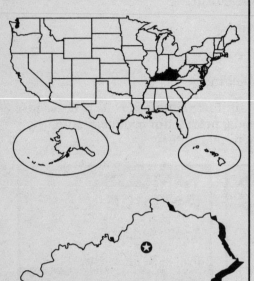

GEOGRAPHY

A southeastern central state, its borders to the north are Illinois, Indiana, and Ohio; its eastern border is West Virginia and Virginia, its western border is Missouri, and its southern border is Tennessee.

KENTUCKY

HISTORY

The name Kentucky comes from an Iroquois Indian word, *ken-tah-ten*, meaning "land of tomorrow." Daniel Boone, a Virginia trader, led the way through the Wilderness Trail. In 1775, Daniel Boone founded Fort Boonesborough. Until the American Revolution, the Indians and British fought continuously. In 1792, Virginia no longer claimed Kentucky, and it became the fifteenth state.

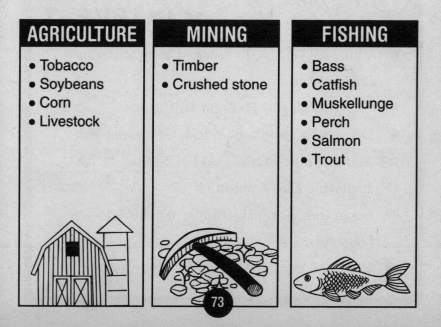

AGRICULTURE

- Tobacco
- Soybeans
- Corn
- Livestock

MINING

- Timber
- Crushed stone

FISHING

- Bass
- Catfish
- Muskellunge
- Perch
- Salmon
- Trout

73

KENTUCKY

SPORTS AND RECREATION

Mountains and reservoirs of Kentucky offer abundant recreational facilities. Rodeos and the Kentucky Derby, one of the world's most famous horse races, are popular attractions. State parks are abundant.

ATTRACTIONS OF INTEREST

☞ Churchill Downs, Kentucky Derby Museum—Louisville

☞ Shaker Village—Pleasant Hill

☞ Dixie Belle Paddle Boat Ride—Pleasant Hill

☞ Mammoth Cave National Park—Canal City

☞ Louisville Zoo—Louisville

☞ Stage One, Kentucky Center for the Arts—Louisville

☞ Rauch Memorial Planetarium—Louisville

ECONOMY

- ⇨ Coal mining
- ⇨ Agriculture
- ⇨ Construction
- ⇨ Manufacturing: non-electrical equipment, electronic products, food products, metals, chemicals, and clothing

1ST

FAMOUS FIRSTS

First permanent settlement of Kentucky—Harrodsburg, 1774
First coal mining—early 1800's
First road in Kentucky— Wilderness road through Cumberland Gap, 1775

FAMOUS PEOPLE

Muhammad Ali

Daniel Boone

Henry Clay

Jefferson Davis

Mary Todd Lincoln

Diane Sawyer

FURTHER INFORMATION

Chamber of Commerce
452 Versailles RD
P.O. Box 817
Frankfort, KY 40602

LOUISIANA

**18th State,
April 30, 1812**

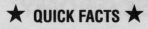

★ QUICK FACTS ★

CAPITAL: Baton Rouge

POPULATION: 4,251,569

AREA: 47,752 sq mi,
ranks 31st

NICKNAME: Sugar State,
Creole State, Pelican
State, and Bayou State

MOTTO: "Union, Justice,
and Confidence"

BIRD: Eastern brown
pelican

TREE: Bald cypress

FLOWER: Magnolia

SONG: "Give Me
Louisiana"

TIME ZONE: Central, DST

HIGHEST POINT: 535 ft,
Driskill Mountain

LOWEST POINT: 5 ft below
sea level, New Orleans

POSTAL ABBREVIATION: LA

GEOGRAPHY

Louisiana has three main land
regions: the East Gulf Coastal Plain, the Mississippi
Alluvial Plain, and the West Gulf Coastal Plain. Its
general coastline is 397 miles along the Gulf of Mexico.
Because of uneven silt deposits, including bays, offshore
islands, and river mouths, its tidal shorelines are 7,721
miles.

HISTORY

The name Louisiana was given to the region by Sieur de La Salle in honor of Louis XIV of France. Early Spanish explorers were Pineda (1519), Cabeza de Vaca (1528), and de Soto (1541). La Salle claimed all the land for Louis XIV of France in 1628. Louisiana was a French crown colony in 1731. In 1763, it was ceded to Spain and in 1800 returned to France, whereby Napoleon sold it to the United States as part of the Louisiana Purchase in 1803.

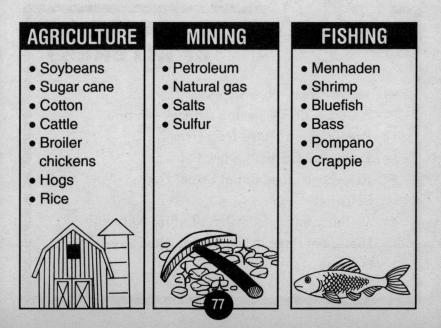

AGRICULTURE

- Soybeans
- Sugar cane
- Cotton
- Cattle
- Broiler chickens
- Hogs
- Rice

MINING

- Petroleum
- Natural gas
- Salts
- Sulfur

FISHING

- Menhaden
- Shrimp
- Bluefish
- Bass
- Pompano
- Crappie

LOUISIANA

SPORTS AND RECREATION

Louisiana is called "sportsman's paradise." Boating, fishing, golfing, hiking, hunting, water sports, and biking are popular sports enjoyed in Louisiana. Football is a favorite spectator sport, including the NFL's New Orleans Saints. The Sugar Bowl game is played at the Superdome each New Year's Day.

ATTRACTIONS OF INTEREST

- ☞ Mardi Gras—New Orleans
- ☞ A Cajun Man's Swamp Cruise—Houma
- ☞ Preservation Hall—New Orleans
- ☞ Zoological Garden—New Orleans
- ☞ Riverboat rides, Canal Street Docks—New Orleans
- ☞ Walking tours, from Jean Lafitte National Historical Park in the French Quarter—New Orleans

ECONOMY

- ⇨ Tourism
- ⇨ Rice
- ⇨ Manufacturing: chemicals, fertilizers, soap, paint, processed food, petroleum, paper, lumber, transportation equipment, and coal products

FAMOUS FIRSTS

The sugar industry began in Louisiana in 1795

The steamboat *New Orleans* completed the first steam-powered trip in 1812

The world's longest bridge—the Lake Ponchartrain Causeway between New Orleans and Mandeville

First bridge across the Mississippi River—Huey Long Bridge, 1935

FAMOUS PEOPLE

Louis Armstrong

Pierre Beauregard

Grace King

Huey Long

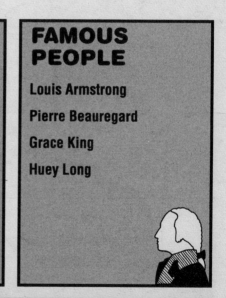

FURTHER INFORMATION

State Dept. of Culture, Recreation and Tourism
P.O. Box 94291
Baton Rouge, LA 70804–9291

MAINE

**23rd State,
March 15, 1820**

★ QUICK FACTS ★

Capital: Augusta

Population: 1,234,602

Area: 33,265 sq mi,
ranks 39th

Nickname: Pine Tree State

Motto: "I Direct"

Bird: Chickadee

Tree: White pine

Flower: White pine cone
and tassel

Song: "State of Maine
Song"

Time Zone: Eastern, DST

Highest Point: 5,268 ft,
Mt. Katahdin

Lowest Point: Sea level,
Atlantic Ocean

Postal Abbreviation: ME

GEOGRAPHY

Maine's northeastern tip borders Canada. The Atlantic
Ocean is to its east; New Hampshire is to its south and
west. The Longfellow Mountains surround Maine. The
major rivers are Androscoggin, Kennebec, and Penobscot.
Sand dunes prevail near Freeport. There are
approximately 3,400 miles of coastline.

HISTORY

This state's name was first used to distinguish the mainland from the offshore islands. Abnaki and Etchemin tribes of the Algonkian Indian family lived in Maine before white people arrived. Vikings visited Maine about A.D. 1000. In 1492, John Cabot explored the Maine coast. In 1607, English settlers established the first colony. In 1677, Massachusetts bought Maine from Ferdinando Gogh's heirs. In the American Revolution, Maine fought at Bunker Hill. In 1820, Maine broke away from Massachusetts and became a separate state.

AGRICULTURE	MINING	FISHING
• Hay	• Sand	• Lobster
• Apples	• Gravel	• Cod
• Potatoes	• Cement	• Menhaden
• Blueberries	• Crushed stone	• Herring
• Livestock		• Pollack

MAINE

SPORTS AND RECREATION

Many tourists flock to Maine for vacationing along its long coastline and many lakes. Water recreation, hunting, fishing, hiking, camping, and boating are popular at the many resorts. Winter offers ski resorts and acres of parks.

ATTRACTIONS OF INTEREST

- ☞ Acadia National Park—47 miles southeast of Bangor
- ☞ Maine Maritime Museum—Bath
- ☞ Maine State Museum—Augusta
- ☞ Wadsworth-Longfellow House—Portland
- ☞ Fishing fleets—Portland
- ☞ Acadian whale watching

ECONOMY

- ⇨ Principal manufactured goods: leather goods, paper products, and wood products

- ⇨ Insurance

- ⇨ Real estate

- ⇨ Services

- ⇨ Trade

- ⇨ Government finance

1ST FAMOUS FIRSTS

Invention of the doughnut hole—Capt. Hanson, 1847

Maine's first industry— shipbuilding, 1607

First naval battle of the Revolution—Machras, 1775

State's first English settlement—the Popham Colony, 1607

Nation's first incorporated city—York, 1641

FAMOUS PEOPLE

Cyrus H. K. Curtis

Hannibal Hamlin

Henry Wadsworth
 Longfellow

Edna St. Vincent Millay

Kate Douglas Wiggins

FURTHER INFORMATION

Chamber of Commerce & Industry
126 Sewall ST
Augusta, ME 04330

MARYLAND

**7th State,
April 28, 1788**

★ QUICK FACTS ★

CAPITAL: Annapolis

POPULATION: 4,859,790

AREA: 10,460 sq mi, ranks 42nd

NICKNAME: Old Line State, Free State

MOTTO: "Manly Deeds, Womanly Words"

BIRD: Baltimore oriole

TREE: White oak

FLOWER: Black-eyed Susan

SONG: "Maryland! My Maryland!"

TIME ZONE: Eastern, DST

HIGHEST POINT: 3,360 ft, Backbone Mountain

LOWEST POINT: Sea level, Atlantic Ocean

POSTAL ABBREVIATION: MD

GEOGRAPHY

Maryland is a mid-Atlantic state with the Atlantic Ocean to its east; Virginia and West Virginia to its southwest; Washington, DC, to its south; and Pennsylvania to its north.

HISTORY

Maryland was first explored in 1608 by Captain John Smith. In 1631, William Clairborne began trading in Kent. That year, Britain gave a charter to Cecil Calvert, Lord Baltimore. Maryland gave up land at its northern boundary, which became the District of Columbia in 1791. During the War of 1812, the British tried to capture Baltimore. It was during the battle at Fort McHenry in 1814 that Francis Scott Key wrote "The Star Spangled Banner."

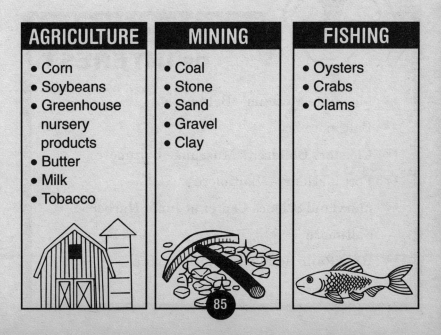

AGRICULTURE

- Corn
- Soybeans
- Greenhouse nursery products
- Butter
- Milk
- Tobacco

MINING

- Coal
- Stone
- Sand
- Gravel
- Clay

FISHING

- Oysters
- Crabs
- Clams

MARYLAND

SPORTS AND RECREATION

Maryland's coastline offers resorts, boardwalks, and water sports at its many beaches. The Baltimore Orioles attract baseball fans to Camden Yards. Golf, horse racing, tennis, biking, hiking, fishing, soccer, and hockey are also options here, as well as many cultural activities offered at its theaters and museums.

ATTRACTIONS OF INTEREST

- ☞ Maritime Museum—Baltimore
- ☞ Baltimore Zoo
- ☞ Cloisters Children's Museum—Baltimore
- ☞ Fort McHenry—Baltimore
- ☞ Maryland Science Center at Inner Harbor— Baltimore
- ☞ B&O Railroad Museum—Baltimore

ECONOMY

⇨ Space research and development

⇨ Manufacturing: electric and electronic equipment, primary metals, chemicals, transportation equipment, printed materials, and food products

1ST

FAMOUS FIRSTS

"The Star Spangled Banner" written here in 1814 by Francis Scott Key

First telegraph line—1844. The words "what hath God wrought" were sent by Samuel Morse from Washington, DC, to Baltimore.

First settlement in Maryland on Kent Island

FAMOUS PEOPLE

Francis Scott Key

Charles W. Peale

William Pinkney

Upton Sinclair

FURTHER INFORMATION

Chamber of Commerce
60 West ST, Suite 405
Annapolis, MD 21410

MASSACHUSETTS

**6th State,
February 6, 1788**

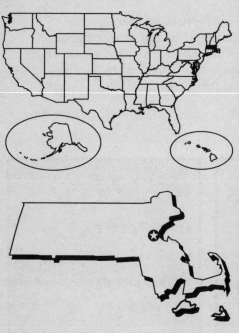

GEOGRAPHY

Massachusetts is bordered on its north by New Hampshire and Vermont, its south by Connecticut and Rhode Island, and its west by New York. Two-thirds of the state abuts the sea. The Connecticut River Valley divides the regions. The Berkshire Hills and Appalachian Mountains cross the western barrier of the state.

HISTORY

Massachusetts gets its name from the Massachusetts Indian tribe, which lived in the region when the Pilgrims arrived. The name means "near the great hill." Pilgrims sailed from Plymouth, England, on the *Mayflower*, on September 16, 1620. That November they landed at what now is Provincetown Harbor. In 1770, the Boston Massacre was the result of British restrictions, as was the Boston Tea Party of 1773. The Revolutionary War began at Lexington in 1775.

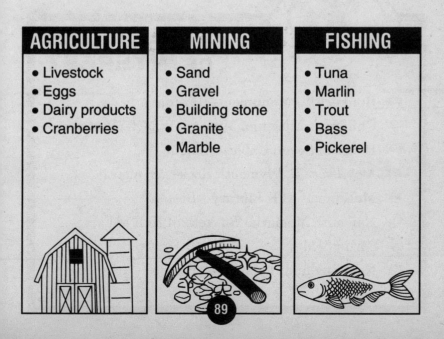

AGRICULTURE	MINING	FISHING
• Livestock	• Sand	• Tuna
• Eggs	• Gravel	• Marlin
• Dairy products	• Building stone	• Trout
• Cranberries	• Granite	• Bass
	• Marble	• Pickerel

MASSACHUSETTS

SPORTS AND RECREATION

Spectator sports include baseball's Boston Red Sox,
football's New England Patriots, the Boston Bruins
hockey team, and basketball's Boston Celtics.
Boating, hiking, walking tours, fishing,
hunting, and water activities are abundant
along the coastline.

ATTRACTIONS OF INTEREST

☞ Bunker Hill Monument—Boston

☞ Children's Museum, Museum Wharf—Boston

☞ House of Seven Gables—Salem

☞ *Mayflower II*, Plymouth Rock—Plymouth

☞ Museum at JFK Library—Boston

☞ Naismith Memorial Basketball Hall of Fame—
Springfield

☞ New England Aquarium—Boston

ECONOMY

- ⇨ Tourism
- ⇨ Numerous colleges
- ⇨ Manufacturing: computer technology, machinery, electric and electronic equipment, instruments, and fabricated metal products
- ⇨ Printing and publishing

1ST

FAMOUS FIRSTS

The sewing machine invented by Elias Howe in 1845

The telephone invented by Alexander Graham Bell in 1876

First public school—The Boston Latin School, 1635

First college—Harvard, 1635

First printing press—The Boston News Letter, 1704

First shots of the Revolutionary War, fired at British troops at Lexington and Concord —April 19, 1775

FAMOUS PEOPLE

John Adams

John Quincy Adams

Louisa May Alcott

Clara Barton

John F. Kennedy

Henry David Thoreau

FURTHER INFORMATION

Massachusetts Office of
Travel & Tourism
100 Cambridge ST
13th Floor
Boston, MA 02202

MICHIGAN

**26th State,
January 26, 1837**

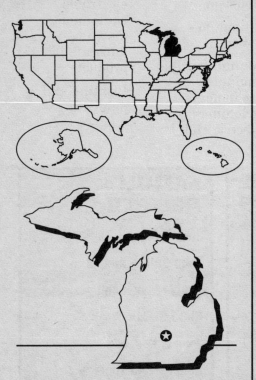

GEOGRAPHY

A northeastern central state
bordering on four of the five
Great Lakes, Michigan is divided into an upper and
lower peninsula by the Straits of Mackinac linking
Lakes Huron and Michigan.

MICHIGAN

HISTORY

The name Michigan comes from two Indian words meaning "Great Lake." Ottawa Indians lived here first. French fur trappers came next. Starting in 1668, the Jesuits established settlements. In 1701, Detroit was established. The British ousted the French, provoking Pontiac's War. The Indians besieged Fort Detroit in 1763. The British were eventually removed by 1813. The Erie Canal opened in 1825. The capital moved from Detroit to Lansing in 1847.

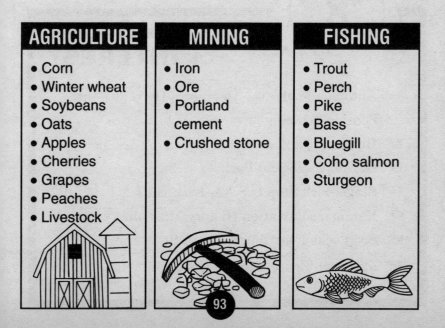

AGRICULTURE	MINING	FISHING
• Corn	• Iron	• Trout
• Winter wheat	• Ore	• Perch
• Soybeans	• Portland	• Pike
• Oats	cement	• Bass
• Apples	• Crushed stone	• Bluegill
• Cherries		• Coho salmon
• Grapes		• Sturgeon
• Peaches		
• Livestock		

MICHIGAN

SPORTS AND RECREATION

Michigan's many miles of freshwater shoreline attract vacationers for water sports. Fishing is popular, as are winter sports and spectator sports, which include professional football's Detroit Lions and basketball's Pistons.

ATTRACTIONS OF INTEREST

☞ Automobile plants—Dearborn, Detroit, Flint, Pontiac, Lansing

☞ Binder Park Zoo—Battle Creek

☞ Detroit Zoological Park

☞ Stagecoach Stop U.S.A.—Irish Hills

☞ Kalamazoo Aviation History Museum

☞ Soo Locks Boat Tours—Sault St. Marie

☞ Michigan Space Center—Jackson

ECONOMY

⇨ Manufacturing: automobile parts and engines, truck trailers, conveyors, sporting equipment, refrigerators, hardware, industrial products, and tires

FAMOUS FIRSTS

First electric battery—Fort Gratiat (Port Huron), 1817
First railroad in Michigan—Erie and Kalamazoo, 1836, 35 miles
First automobile—1896, Henry Ford
First automobile factory—1899, Ranson Olds

FAMOUS PEOPLE

Gerald Ford

Henry Ford

Aretha Franklin

Lee Iacocca

Earvin "Magic" Johnson

Charles Lindbergh

Malcom X

Stevie Wonder

FURTHER INFORMATION

Chamber of Commerce
200 N. Washington SQ
Suite 400
Lansing, MI 48933

MINNESOTA

**32nd State,
May 11, 1858**

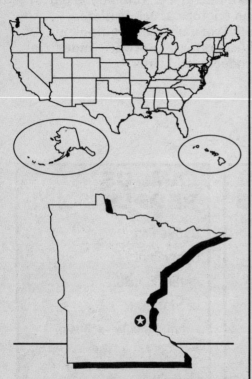

GEOGRAPHY

A northern central state, Minnesota borders on its
east Wisconsin and Lake Superior; on its north is
Canada, west is North and South Dakota, and south
is Iowa.

HISTORY

The name Minnesota comes from a
Dakota Indian word meaning "sky-tinted
water." In 1679, Louis XIV claimed this land.
The United States bought part of Minnesota
from the English after the Revolutionary War and the
western part from France after the Louisiana Purchase.
The land had belonged to the Sioux in the seventeenth and
eighteenth centuries. The Sioux resented the treatment by
the settlers, and there were many casualties on both sides.
The Sioux were defeated and fled toward the Dakotas and
Missouri.

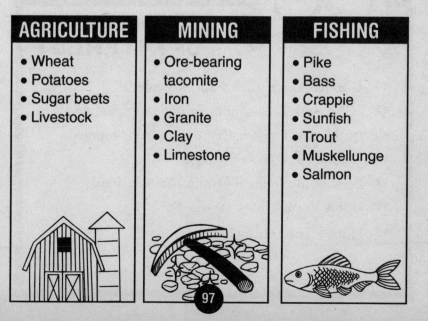

AGRICULTURE

- Wheat
- Potatoes
- Sugar beets
- Livestock

MINING

- Ore-bearing
  tacomite
- Iron
- Granite
- Clay
- Limestone

FISHING

- Pike
- Bass
- Crappie
- Sunfish
- Trout
- Muskellunge
- Salmon

MINNESOTA

SPORTS AND RECREATION

Water sports are popular because of the vast mileage of water. Canoe trails mapping Indian trails are popular. Fishing, hiking, snowmobiling, sledding, and downhill and cross-country skiing are available.

ATTRACTIONS OF INTEREST

- ☞ U.S. Hockey Hall of Fame—Eveleth
- ☞ Minnesota Zoo—Apple Valley
- ☞ Children's Theater Company—Minneapolis
- ☞ Combo Park Zoo—St. Paul
- ☞ Science Museum of Minnesota—St. Paul
- ☞ Gibbs Farm Museum—St. Paul
- ☞ Hubert Humphrey Metrodome

ECONOMY

⇨ Tourism

⇨ Publishing calendars and law books

⇨ Manufacturing: computers, electronic equipment, computer hardware and software, textiles, sporting goods, farm machinery, and plastics

1ST

FAMOUS FIRSTS

First ore mined from the Vermilion Range, 1884

First lumberjacks—1830's, began cutting lumber

First flour mill—Falls of St. Anthony, 1823

Record balloon flight—1957, 32 hours in the air

FAMOUS PEOPLE

F. Scott Fitzgerald

Hubert Humphrey

Charles Mayo

Walter Mondale

Charles Schultz

? FURTHER INFORMATION

Minnesota Office of Tourism
375 Jackson ST
250 Skyway Level
St. Paul, MN 55101

MISSISSIPPI

**20th State,
December 10, 1817**

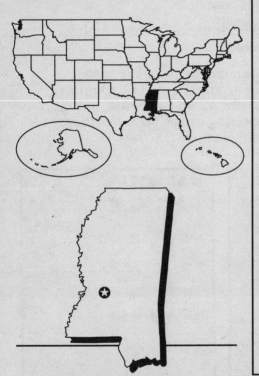

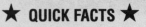

★ QUICK FACTS ★

CAPITAL: Jackson

POPULATION: 2,592,003

AREA: 47,689 sq mi, ranks 32nd

NICKNAME: Magnolia State

MOTTO: "By Valor and Arms"

BIRD: Mockingbird

TREE: Magnolia

FLOWER: Magnolia

SONG: "Go, Mississippi"

TIME ZONE: Central, DST

HIGHEST POINT: 806 ft, Woodall Mountain

LOWEST POINT: Sea level, Gulf of Mexico

POSTAL ABBREVIATION: MS

GEOGRAPHY

A southern state bordered on the south by the Gulf of Mexico and on the west by the Mississippi River, Mississippi has a low fertile delta, sandy gulf coastal territory, and high hills in the northeast.

HISTORY

Spain first explored Mississippi. Hernando de Soto discovered the Mississippi River in 1540. The French first settled near Biloxi in 1699. In 1763, Great Britain won the land in the French and Indian War, leaving it to the United States in 1783 after the Revolution. In the 1900's, agriculture, industry, and education progressed. County agricultural high schools were established in 1908. Mississippi retains many reminders of the Old South with its antebellum mansions and plantations.

AGRICULTURE

- Cotton
- Soybeans
- Rice
- Livestock

MINING

- Petroleum
- Natural gas
- Sand
- Gravel
- Stone

FISHING

- Bass
- Bream
- Catfish
- Shrimp
- Menhaden
- Trout
- Perch

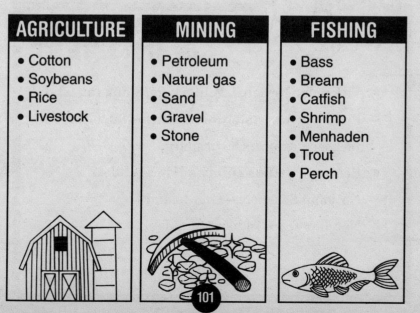

MISSISSIPPI

SPORTS AND RECREATION

The Gulf Coast, including Biloxi, Ocean Springs, Pascagoula, and Pass Christian, offers sandy beaches and water sports. The historic Old Spanish Trail connects the resort cities. Fishing, hunting, camping, and hiking are available activities.

ATTRACTIONS OF INTEREST

☞ Vicksburg National Military Park and Cemetery

☞ Pre-Civil War stately old homes—Natchez, Jackson, Oxford, Hattiesburg

☞ Beauvoir, Jefferson Davis Home—Biloxi

☞ National Seashore—Gulf Island

☞ Natchez Trace Indian Mounds

ECONOMY

- ⇨ Food processing
- ⇨ Seafood
- ⇨ Apparel
- ⇨ Furniture
- ⇨ Lumber and wood products
- ⇨ Electrical machinery and equipment
- ⇨ Transportation equipment
- ⇨ Petroleum and coal products

1ST FAMOUS FIRSTS

The petroleum industry developed in Mississippi in 1939

Mississippi's first colony—Old Biloxi, settled by the French in 1699

Cottonseed oil industry—established in Natchez in the 1870's

FAMOUS PEOPLE

Hodding Carter III

Medgar Evers

William Faulkner

Fannie Lou Hamer

Charlie Pride

Tennessee Williams

Oprah Winfrey

FURTHER INFORMATION

Chamber of Commerce
P.O. Box 1849
Jackson, MS 39205

MISSOURI

**24th State,
August 10, 1821**

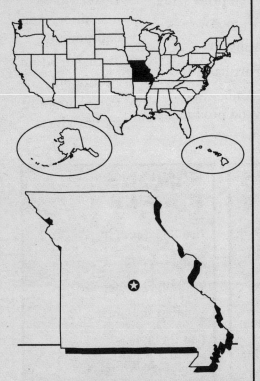

★ **QUICK FACTS** ★

CAPITAL: Jefferson City

POPULATION: 5,219,000

AREA: 69,697 sq mi,
ranks 19th

NICKNAME: Show Me State

MOTTO: "The Welfare of
the People Shall Be the
Supreme Law"

BIRD: Bluebird

TREE: Flowering dogwood

FLOWER: Hawthorne

SONG: "Missouri Waltz"

TIME ZONE: Central, DST

HIGHEST POINT: 1,772 ft,
Taum Sauk Mountain

LOWEST POINT: 230 ft,
St. Frances River

POSTAL ABBREVIATION: MO

GEOGRAPHY

Located in the midwestern central United States,
Missouri is bordered on the east by the Mississippi
River and on the northwest by the Missouri River.
With rolling hills (Missouri Ozarks) and fertile
plains, it is prairies north of the Missouri River,
while rough and hilly south of the river.

HISTORY

The name Missouri came from the Indian word meaning the "town of the large canoes." Hernando de Soto visited Missouri in 1541. In 1682, Sieur de La Salle captured it for France; French fur trading began. St. Louis was first settled in 1764. Missouri became part of the United States with the Louisiana Purchase in 1803. The state remained in the Union during the Civil War. St. Joseph was the starting point of the Pony Express.

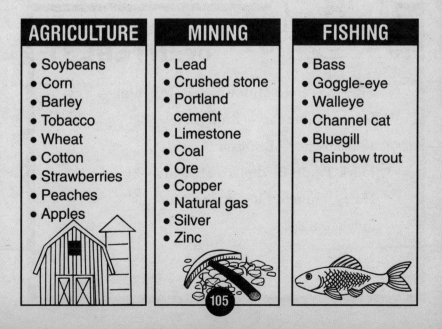

AGRICULTURE

- Soybeans
- Corn
- Barley
- Tobacco
- Wheat
- Cotton
- Strawberries
- Peaches
- Apples

MINING

- Lead
- Crushed stone
- Portland cement
- Limestone
- Coal
- Ore
- Copper
- Natural gas
- Silver
- Zinc

FISHING

- Bass
- Goggle-eye
- Walleye
- Channel cat
- Bluegill
- Rainbow trout

MISSOURI

SPORTS AND RECREATION

Resort communities are Lake Ozark and Osage Beach, Branson, and Rockaway Beach on Bull Shoals Lake. There are many water sports available in the south-central parts of this state. Many outdoor activities are found in the Ozarks. Camping, hiking, hunting, and fishing are popular.

ATTRACTIONS OF INTEREST

☞ Six Flags Over Mid-America—Allenton

☞ Silver Dollar City—Branson

☞ White Water—Branson

☞ Mark Twain Birthplace Museum—Florida

☞ Harry Truman Library and Museum—Independence

ECONOMY

- ⇨ Manufacturing: electrical and electronic equipment, transportation equipment, and chemicals
- ⇨ Aerospace
- ⇨ Tourism
- ⇨ Food and related products
- ⇨ Shoes
- ⇨ Lead

FAMOUS FIRSTS

The Dred Scott decision made by the Supreme Court in 1857

First permanent settlement in Missouri region—Ste. Genevieve, 1735

FAMOUS PEOPLE

Dale Carnegie

Walter Cronkite

Walt Disney

Jesse James

Meriwether Lewis and

William Clark

Harry Truman

FURTHER INFORMATION

Chamber of Commerce
400 E. High ST
P.O. Box 149
Jefferson City, MO 65101

MONTANA

**41st State,
November 8, 1889**

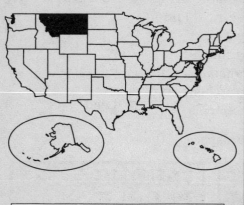

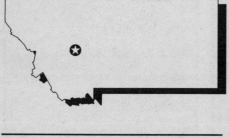

GEOGRAPHY

Montana is a mountain state that is bounded on the east by North and South Dakota, on the north by Canada, on the south by Wyoming, and the west/southwest by Idaho.

HISTORY

Montana is a Latin-Spanish word meaning "mountainous." In the 1850's the cattle industry began. Ranching continued to prevail here even after blizzards killed many cattle. A wealth of gold and silver was discovered in the mountains of Montana in 1862. The last stand of General George Custer and the final battle of the Nez Percé Wars were fought here. Butte once supplied half of U.S. copper. Today Montana develops agriculture and mineral products.

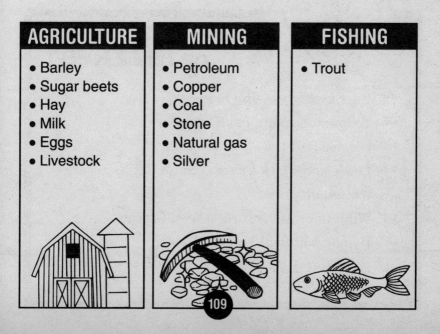

AGRICULTURE

- Barley
- Sugar beets
- Hay
- Milk
- Eggs
- Livestock

MINING

- Petroleum
- Copper
- Coal
- Stone
- Natural gas
- Silver

FISHING

- Trout

MONTANA

SPORTS AND RECREATION

Montana is a popular vacation state of vast beauty, whose national parks, and rivers and lakes offer fishing, swimming, boating, trail riding, mountain climbing, and rafting. Winter sports are available November through April.

ATTRACTIONS OF INTEREST

- ☞ Big Sky Resort—Big Sky
- ☞ Yellowstone National Park
- ☞ Glacier Raft Co.—Nevada City
- ☞ Lewis and Clark Caverns State Park—Whitehall
- ☞ Wild River Adventures—West Glacier
- ☞ Helena National Forest—Helena
- ☞ Glacier National Park

ECONOMY

- Agriculture
- Timber
- Tourism
- Oil and gas
- Manufacturing: food products, wood and paper goods, metals, petroleum and coal products
- Printing and publishing

FAMOUS FIRSTS

Cattle industry began in Montana in 1850

First crops—wheat and potatoes

Oil production began in 1915 in the Williston Basin

FAMOUS PEOPLE

Gary Cooper

Marcus Daly

Chet Huntley

Will James

Myrna Loy

Mike Mansfield

FURTHER INFORMATION

Chamber of Commerce
2030 11th AVE
P.O. Box 1730
Helena, MT 59624

NEBRASKA

**37th State,
March 1, 1867**

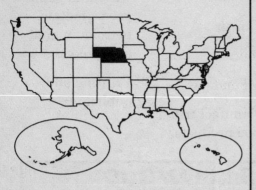

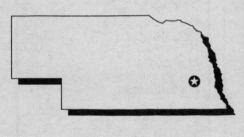

GEOGRAPHY

A midwestern state, Nebraska is bordered by South Dakota to the north, Iowa and Missouri to the east, Kansas to the south, and Colorado and Wyoming to the west.

HISTORY

The name Nebraska comes from the Oto Indian word meaning "flat water." Prior to the Louisiana Purchase, French and Spanish explorers traveled through what is now Nebraska. The first permanent settlement was Bellevue, near Omaha, in 1823. The Homestead Act, providing grants of public lands, caused many battles between homesteaders and ranchers. European immigrants migrated to Nebraska between 1860 and 1890. They brought with them their customs and skills. The Cheyenne, Sioux, and Pawnee Indians, led by war chiefs Crazy Horse, Dull Knife, and Red Cloud, battled against the new Nebraskans but were defeated.

AGRICULTURE

- Corn
- Wheat
- Soybeans
- Grain
- Sugar
- Hay
- Livestock

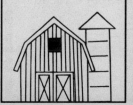

MINING

- Petroleum
- Sand
- Gravel
- Natural gas
- Oil
- Crushed stone

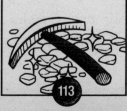

FISHING

- Rainbow and brown trout
- Walleye
- Pike
- Catfish
- Crappie
- Perch
- Bass

NEBRASKA

SPORTS AND RECREATION

Nebraska offers water sports such as boating, swimming, canoeing, rafting, and water-skiing on its many lakes and reservoirs. Hiking, riding, camping, and picnicking are available at Nebraska's National Forest and in central Nebraska.

ATTRACTIONS OF INTEREST

☞ Grand Island Heritage Zoo

☞ Stuhr Museum of the Prairie Pioneers—Grand Island

☞ Folsom Children's Zoo—Lincoln

☞ University of Nebraska State Museum—Lincoln

☞ Ak-Sar-Ben Coliseum—Omaha

☞ Omaha Children's Museum

ECONOMY

⇨ Manufacturing: electronic components, food products, chemicals, pharmaceuticals, mobile homes, and transportation equipment

⇨ Food processing

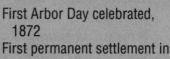

FAMOUS FIRSTS

First Arbor Day celebrated, 1872

First permanent settlement in Nebraska—Bellevue, 1823

FAMOUS PEOPLE

Fred Astaire

Johnny Carson

Buffalo Bill (William F.) Cody

Henry Fonda

Red Cloud

FURTHER INFORMATION

Chamber of Commerce
1320 Lincoln Mall
P.O. Box 95128
Lincoln, NE 68501

NEVADA

**36th State,
October 31, 1864**

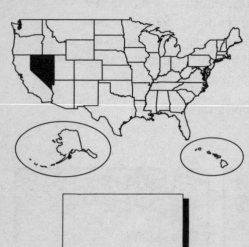

CAPITAL: Carson City

POPULATION: 1,102,000

AREA: 109,540 sq mi, ranks 7th

NICKNAME: Silver State, Sagebrush State, Battle-born State

MOTTO: "All for Our Country"

BIRD: Mountain bluebird

TREE: Bristlecone pine, single-leaf

FLOWER: Sagebrush

SONG: "Home Means Nevada"

TIME ZONE: Pacific, DST

HIGHEST POINT: 13,143 ft, Boundary Peak, White Mountains

LOWEST POINT: 470 ft, along the Colorado River

POSTAL ABBREVIATION: NV

GEOGRAPHY

Nevada lies almost entirely within the Great Basin. It is a huge desert area extending to Oregon, Idaho, Wyoming, California, and Utah.

HISTORY

Nevada was acquired by the United States in 1848. Explored by Spaniards in 1776, its first settlement was Mormon Station, now known as Genoa. During the gold rush people en route to California thought they discovered gold in Nevada at the mouth of Gold Canyon in the 1850's. It was actually silver ore and became known as the Comstock Lode. Originally part of Utah territory, in 1861 it became a territory in its own right.

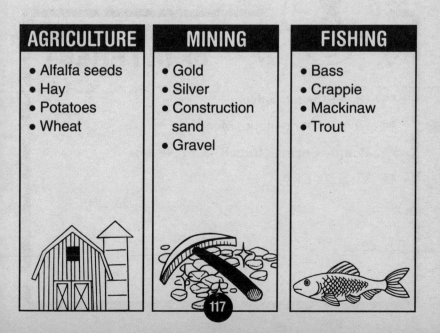

AGRICULTURE

- Alfalfa seeds
- Hay
- Potatoes
- Wheat

MINING

- Gold
- Silver
- Construction sand
- Gravel

FISHING

- Bass
- Crappie
- Mackinaw
- Trout

NEVADA

SPORTS AND RECREATION

Besides live entertainment, outdoor recreation is available in water sports on the lakes, golf, horseback riding, mountain climbing, and skiing. Lake Tahoe is a popular recreational center near Reno. Lake Mead Recreational Area and Mt. Charleston serve Las Vegas.

ATTRACTIONS OF INTEREST

- ☞ Ghost towns, rodeos
- ☞ Hoover Dam—Lake Mead
- ☞ Bonnie Springs Ranch—Old Nevada
- ☞ Virginia City

ECONOMY

⇨ Tourism

⇨ Gambling

⇨ Mining

⇨ Manufacturing: chemicals and aerospace products

⇨ Agriculture

FAMOUS FIRSTS

Comstock Lode—Gold and silver discovered in Virginia City, 1859

First federal irrigation project—Newlands Project, 1907 (along Carson and Truckee Rivers)

First transcontinental railroad system—Central Pacific, through the Sierra Mountains into Nevada in the 1860's

FAMOUS PEOPLE

Kit Carson

Walter Van Tilburg Clark

John C. Tremont

FURTHER INFORMATION

Commission on Tourism
Capitol Complex
Carson City, NV 89710

NEW HAMPSHIRE

**9th State,
June 21, 1788**

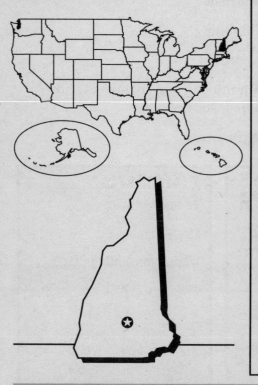

GEOGRAPHY

Bounded on the south by Massachusetts, the west by Vermont, the northwest by Canada, and the east by Maine and the Atlantic Ocean, New Hampshire has a long coastline, with mountains and hills. New Hampshire is known for its beautiful scenery, which includes the White Mountains.

NEW HAMPSHIRE

HISTORY

New Hampshire's first settlement was Odiorne Point in Rye (1623). Border disputes among different religious groups went on for a century. John Mason gave the territory the name New Hampshire. New Hampshire was forced to unite with Massachusetts for several years until a legislative body was established. During the 1800's New Hampshire became less of an agricultural state. Factories and mills were built. Many laborers came from Europe and Canada to work in these mills and factories.

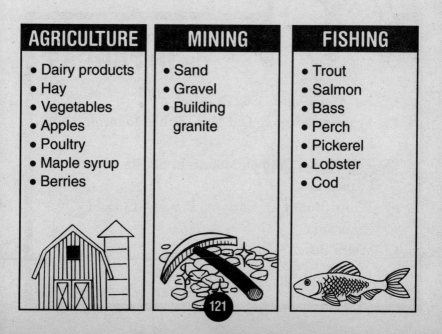

AGRICULTURE

- Dairy products
- Hay
- Vegetables
- Apples
- Poultry
- Maple syrup
- Berries

MINING

- Sand
- Gravel
- Building granite

FISHING

- Trout
- Salmon
- Bass
- Perch
- Pickerel
- Lobster
- Cod

NEW HAMPSHIRE

SPORTS AND RECREATION

Water sports abound on the coastline with its many beaches. The White Mountains are a major vacation attraction with lakes offering popular recreation centers. Winter provides skiing, ice fishing, and snowshoeing. Camping, fishing, and hunting are also popular sports.

ATTRACTIONS OF INTEREST

- ☞ Mt. Washington Cog Railway
- ☞ Franconia Notch, Old Man of the Mountains—Franconia
- ☞ Echo Lake, Cannon Mountain Ski Resort—Franconia
- ☞ White Mountain National Forest—Lincoln, Franconia
- ☞ Weirs Beach
- ☞ Lake Winnepesauke—Meredith

NEW HAMPSHIRE

ECONOMY

⇨ Manufacturing: electrical and electronic products, machinery, plastics, fabricated metal products, footwear, and other leather goods

⇨ Tourism

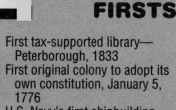

FAMOUS FIRSTS

First tax-supported library—Peterborough, 1833

First original colony to adopt its own constitution, January 5, 1776

U.S. Navy's first shipbuilding yard opened at Portsmouth in 1800

First wagon and coaches to be used to carry passengers and mail—Concord Wagon & Coach, 1813

First cotton mill—New Ipswich, 1804

FAMOUS PEOPLE

Mary Baker Eddy

Robert Frost

Christa McAuliffe

Franklin Pierce

Alan B. Shepard

Daniel Webster

FURTHER INFORMATION

Office of Vacation Travel
172 Pembroke RD
P.O. Box 856
Concord, NH 03301

NEW JERSEY

**3rd State,
December 18, 1787**

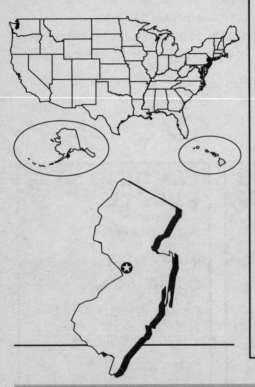

★ QUICK FACTS ★

CAPITAL: Trenton

POPULATION: 7,971,000

AREA: 7,836 sq mi, ranks 46th

NICKNAME: Garden State

MOTTO: "Liberty and Prosperity"

BIRD: Eastern goldfinch

TREE: Red oak

FLOWER: Purple violet

SONG: None

TIME ZONE: Eastern, DST

HIGHEST POINT: 1,803 ft

LOWEST POINT: Sea level, Atlantic Ocean

POSTAL ABBREVIATION: NJ

GEOGRAPHY

A mid-Atlantic state bordered on its north by New York and its east by the Atlantic Ocean, New Jersey's southern border abuts Delaware, and on its west is Pennsylvania.

HISTORY

The name New Jersey comes from the Channel Island of Jersey, which is located between England and France. New Jersey was part of New York. In 1664, New Jersey became an English colony. Fighting occurred here during the American Revolution because of its closeness to New York City and Philadelphia. Today New Jersey is an industrial state known as the crossroads of the East. Considered by many an ideal vacation state, New Jersey has become quite a popular Middle Atlantic State.

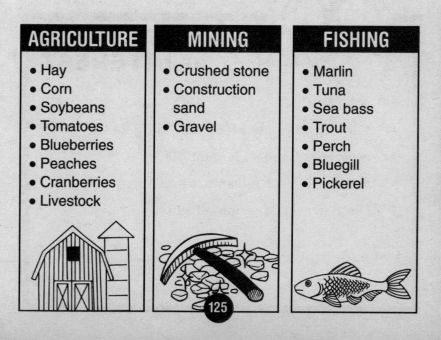

AGRICULTURE	MINING	FISHING
• Hay	• Crushed stone	• Marlin
• Corn	• Construction sand	• Tuna
• Soybeans	• Gravel	• Sea bass
• Tomatoes		• Trout
• Blueberries		• Perch
• Peaches		• Bluegill
• Cranberries		• Pickerel
• Livestock		

NEW JERSEY

SPORTS AND RECREATION

The New Jersey coastline, with its beaches and boardwalks, attracts vacationers. Water sports, including white-water rafting (Delaware Gap National Recreation Area) and fishing are available. Winter offers skiing and other winter activities in northern New Jersey. Spectator sports include N.J. Nets basketball and N.J. Devils hockey.

ATTRACTIONS OF INTEREST

- ☞ Atlantic City
- ☞ Lucy the Margate Elephant—Margate City
- ☞ Storybook Land—Pleasantville
- ☞ Six Flags Great Adventure—Jackson
- ☞ Old Barracks Museum—Trenton

ECONOMY

⇨ Manufacturing: chemicals, electronic and electrical equipment, non-electrical machinery, fabricated metals, pharmaceuticals, textiles, clothing, leather, refined oil, and transportation equipment

1ST FAMOUS FIRSTS

New Jersey was the first state to help local communities build roads (1891)

George Washington Bridge—one of world's longest suspension bridges (1898)

Inventions—electronic telegraph, electric light bulb (1879), submarine (1898)

First game of organized baseball—Hoboken, 1846

First dinosaur skeleton discovered in North America was found buried in Haddonfield

First intercollegiate football game—Rutgers defeated Princeton, 1869

First boardwalk—Atlantic City

FAMOUS PEOPLE

Count Basie

Grover Cleveland

James Fenimore Cooper

David Dinkins

Albert Einstein

Alexander Hamilton

Samuel F.B. Morse

Frank Sinatra

Bruce Springsteen

FURTHER INFORMATION

Chamber of Commerce
51 Commerce ST
Newark, NJ 07102

NEW MEXICO

**47th State,
January 6, 1912**

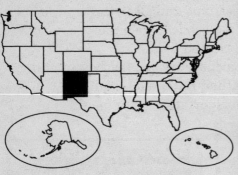

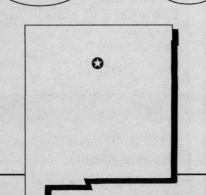

GEOGRAPHY

New Mexico is a southwestern state with Colorado on its north; Oklahoma, Texas, and Mexico to the east and south; and Arizona on its west.

HISTORY

The name New Mexico originates from the country of Mexico. Francisco Vásquez de Coronado, a Spanish explorer looking for gold, discovered New Mexico in 1539. Trade on the Santa Fe Trail to Missouri began in 1821. The Mexican War began in May of 1846. Geronimo's surrender ended the Apache Wars and Indian conflicts in 1886. Today New Mexico is a leading center of space and nuclear research. Its vast mineral reserves assure the state a part in future energy crises.

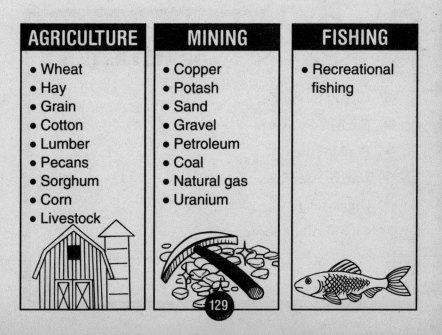

AGRICULTURE	MINING	FISHING
• Wheat	• Copper	• Recreational fishing
• Hay	• Potash	
• Grain	• Sand	
• Cotton	• Gravel	
• Lumber	• Petroleum	
• Pecans	• Coal	
• Sorghum	• Natural gas	
• Corn	• Uranium	
• Livestock		

SPORTS AND RECREATION

Several state forests and parks offer activities. Hiking, riding, camping, and cave exploring are popular. Native American reservations hold many celebrations. State fairs, hot-air balloon fiestas, and art festivals are popular.

ATTRACTIONS OF INTEREST

- ☞ City of Sante Fe
- ☞ Carlsbad Caverns
- ☞ Pueblo ruins
- ☞ Native American reservations
- ☞ Ghost towns
- ☞ City of Albuquerque

ECONOMY

⇨ Tourism

⇨ Agriculture

⇨ Extractive industries

⇨ Manufacturing: foods, electrical machinery, lumber, apparel, and transportation equipment

1ST FAMOUS FIRSTS

First atomic bomb tested— Los Alamos, 1945

First goods brought to Santa Fe from Missouri—Santa Fe Trail, a new trade route

First U.S. road—El Camino Real, 1581, runs from Santa Fe to Chihuahua, Mexico (now known as Highway 85)

FAMOUS PEOPLE

William Bonney (Billy the Kid)

Kit Carson

Nancy Lopez

Georgia O'Keeffe

Lew Wallace

? FURTHER INFORMATION

New Mexico Dept. of Tourism
P.O. Box 20003
Santa Fe, NM 87503

NEW YORK

**11th State,
July 26, 1788**

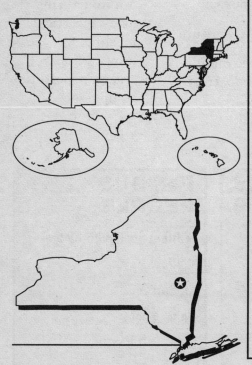

GEOGRAPHY

New York borders Pennsylvania, Vermont, Massachusetts, Connecticut, and Canada to the north. New York's topography is diverse. A narrow lake plain skirts Lake Erie and Lake Ontario. Half of the rest of the state lies in the Appalachian Highland Plateau. Principal rivers are the St. Lawrence, Hudson, Mohawk, and Niagara.

HISTORY

The Algonkian and Iroquois, two of the largest and most powerful Indian groups in North America, lived in New York. In 1524, Giovanni da Verrazano reached New York Bay. In 1609, Henry Hudson, an Englishman working for the Dutch, sailed what is now called the Hudson River. The Netherlands claimed the territories of New York and surrounding areas as New Netherland. Explorer Samuel de Champlain claimed part of New York for France. In 1626, Peter Minuit, a Dutch governor, bought Manhattan from the Indians for trinkets worth twenty-four dollars. In 1624, the English renamed the territory New York after the Duke of York, who later become King James II of England. France and England fought for New York from 1689 until 1763. The Treaty of Paris, signed in 1763, finally ended the wars. By 1850, New York was called the Empire State.

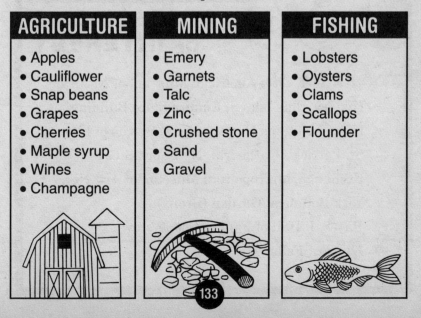

AGRICULTURE

- Apples
- Cauliflower
- Snap beans
- Grapes
- Cherries
- Maple syrup
- Wines
- Champagne

MINING

- Emery
- Garnets
- Talc
- Zinc
- Crushed stone
- Sand
- Gravel

FISHING

- Lobsters
- Oysters
- Clams
- Scallops
- Flounder

NEW YORK

SPORTS AND RECREATION

The eastern half of Long Island and its barrier isle, Fire Island, are lined with beaches and summer resorts. The Adirondacks host numerous resorts, with facilities for hiking, fishing, boating, hunting, and skiing. Lake Placid is a famous ski center. New York hosts more professional spectator sports than any other state. Included are baseball: Mets, Yankees; hockey: Rangers, Islanders; football: Buffalo Bills; basketball: Knickerbockers.

ATTRACTIONS OF INTEREST

☞ New York City: American Museum of Natural History, Ellis Island, Empire State Building, United Nations Headquarters, Statue of Liberty, St. Patrick's Cathedral, New York Stock Exchange, Metropolitan Museum of Art, New York Botanical Garden (Bronx)

☞ Baseball Hall of Fame—Cooperstown

☞ Niagara Falls

ECONOMY

- Tourism
- Financial capital of the nation
- Importing and exporting through port of New York and New Jersey
- Printing and publishing
- Manufacturing: clothing, leather and leather products, electrical and electronic products, chemicals, and machinery

FAMOUS FIRSTS

New York City served as the first capital of the United States from January 11, 1758, to March 2, 1789. George Washington was inaugurated as the nation's first President at Federal Hall in New York City.

First successful steamboat—Robert Fulton's *Clermont*

First woman suffrage convention in United States was organized in Seneca Falls in 1848.

FAMOUS PEOPLE

Millard Fillmore

Jay Gould

J. P. Morgan

Franklin Delano Roosevelt

Theodore Roosevelt

Martin Van Buren

Cornelius Vanderbilt

FURTHER INFORMATION

Dept. of Economic Development
Division of Tourism
One Commerce Plaza
Albany, NY 12245

NORTH CAROLINA

**12th State,
November 21, 1789**

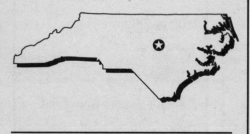

★ QUICK FACTS ★

CAPITAL: Raleigh

POPULATION: 6,736,827

AREA: 52,669 sq mi, ranks 28th

NICKNAME: Tar Heel State, Old North State

MOTTO: "To Be Rather Than to Seem"

BIRD: Cardinal

TREE: Pine

FLOWER: Flowering dogwood

SONG: "The Old North State"

TIME ZONE: Eastern, DST

HIGHEST POINT: 6,684 ft, Mt. Mitchell

LOWEST POINT: Sea level, Atlantic Ocean

POSTAL ABBREVIATION: NC

GEOGRAPHY

A southern Atlantic state, North Carolina is bounded by Virginia, South Carolina, Georgia, Tennessee, and the Atlantic Ocean.

NORTH CAROLINA

HISTORY

North Carolina was named in honor of Charles I of England. The first colonies were settled by the English. Spanish and French explorers passed through North Carolina. In 1587, Raleigh was established. Settlers came from Virginia in 1660. North Carolina was the next-to-the-last state to ratify the Constitution (1789).

AGRICULTURE
- Tobacco
- Soybeans
- Corn
- Peanuts
- Sweet potatoes
- Feed grain
- Fruits
- Vegetables
- Livestock

MINING
- Clay
- Sand
- Gravel
- Crushed stone

FISHING
- Bass
- Trout
- Northern pike

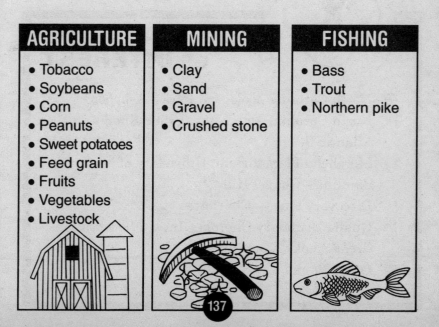

NORTH CAROLINA

SPORTS AND RECREATION

Miles of beaches offer water sports, camping, fishing, and hiking. Undeveloped barrier islands can be reached by ferries, with over forty shipwrecks for scuba divers. North Carolina's several forests and parks offer horseback riding, skiing, and hang gliding. Spectator sports include Charlotte Motor Speedway and World Stock Car Races.

ATTRACTIONS OF INTEREST

- ☞ North Carolina Zoological Park—Asheboro
- ☞ North Carolina Aquarium at Pine Knoll—Atlantic Beach
- ☞ Morehead Planetarium, University of North Carolina—Chapel Hill
- ☞ Discovery Place—Charlotte
- ☞ Qualla Boundary Cherokee Indian Reservation, Great Smoky Mountains
- ☞ Outer Banks

ECONOMY

⇨ Tourism

⇨ Manufacturing: furniture, textiles, chemicals, allied products, hosiery, electrical machinery, paper, handicrafts, basketry, woodcarving, and weaving

1ST

FAMOUS FIRSTS

First airplane flight—Kitty Hawk, December 17, 1903 (Wright Brothers)
First child born to English parents in America— Virginia Dare, 1587
First state university to hold classes—University of North Carolina, 1795

FAMOUS PEOPLE

David Brinkley

Billy Graham

Andrew Johnson

William Rufus King

Dolley Madison

James Polk

FURTHER INFORMATION

Division of Tourism
P.O. Box 25249
Raleigh, NC 27611

NORTH DAKOTA

**34th State,
November 2, 1889**

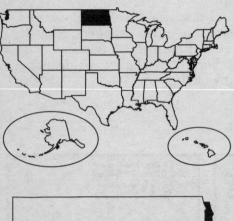

GEOGRAPHY

A northern state situated in the middle of North America, North Dakota is bordered on the north by Canada, east by Minnesota, south by South Dakota, and west by Montana.

HISTORY

North Dakota's name originates from the Sioux Indian word meaning "allies" or "friends." In 1738, French Canadians explored North Dakota. In 1803, the United States acquired most of North Dakota from France as part of the Louisiana Purchase. President Thomas Jefferson sent Lewis and Clark to blaze a trail to the Pacific Ocean. In 1863, the territories of North and South Dakota and much of Montana and Wyoming were opened to homesteading.

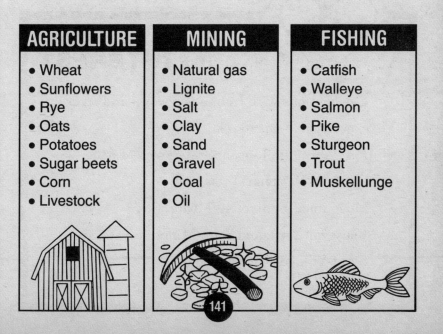

AGRICULTURE

- Wheat
- Sunflowers
- Rye
- Oats
- Potatoes
- Sugar beets
- Corn
- Livestock

MINING

- Natural gas
- Lignite
- Salt
- Clay
- Sand
- Gravel
- Coal
- Oil

FISHING

- Catfish
- Walleye
- Salmon
- Pike
- Sturgeon
- Trout
- Muskellunge

NORTH DAKOTA

SPORTS AND RECREATION

Boating, swimming, and water sports are popular along Lakes Sakakaewa and Oahe. Skiing, snowmobiling, skating, and other winter sports are popular. Camping, hiking, and horseback riding are available.

ATTRACTIONS OF INTEREST

☞ Celebrations with Indian powwows and river expositions—Bismarck

☞ Fort Abraham Lincoln State Park—Little Missouri National Grassland

☞ Museum of Badlands—Medora

☞ Roosevelt Park and Zoo—Minot

☞ Slant Village—Mandan

NORTH DAKOTA

ECONOMY

⇨ Tourism

⇨ Manufacturing: farm equipment, processed foods, furniture, medical equipment, and aerospace equipment

1ST FAMOUS FIRSTS

First Scottish and Irish settlement—Pembina Ranching began in North Dakota in 1800's; Texas cattle fattened-up here

FAMOUS PEOPLE

Tom Brokaw

Louis L'Amour

Peggy Lee

Eric Sevareid

Lawrence Welk

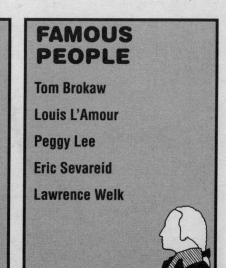

FURTHER INFORMATION

Chamber of Commerce
P.O. Box 2467
Fargo, ND 58108

OHIO

**17th State,
March 1, 1803**

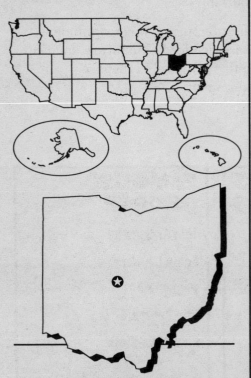

★ QUICK FACTS ★

CAPITAL: Columbus

POPULATION: 10,792,000

AREA: 41,330 sq mi, ranks 35th

NICKNAME: Buckeye State

MOTTO: "With God, All Things Are Possible"

BIRD: Cardinal

TREE: Buckeye

FLOWER: Scarlet carnation

SONG: "Beautiful Ohio"

TIME ZONE: Eastern, DST

HIGHEST POINT: 1,550 ft, Campbell Hill, Bellefontaine

LOWEST POINT: 433 ft, Ohio River

POSTAL ABBREVIATION: OH

GEOGRAPHY

Ohio is a northeastern central state, bordered on its north by Lake Michigan and Lake Erie; east and south by Pennsylvania, West Virginia, and Kentucky; and west by Indiana.

HISTORY

The name Ohio comes from an
Iroquoian word meaning "something
great." After the French and Indian War,
Ohio became a British territory in 1763. Ohio
was acquired by the United States after the Revolutionary
War in 1783 and 1788. It is known as the Buckeye State
because of the buckeye trees that grew in abundance. Lake
Erie's harbors have been an excellent resource for world
commerce. Ohio controlled Lake Erie during the War of
1812. Industrialism contributed to the economy by the end
of the 1800's. Today, nearly four-fifths of the leading
industries in the nation are found in Ohio.

AGRICULTURE

- Hay
- Oats
- Soybeans
- Wheat
- Corn
- Wines
- Dairy farming

MINING

- Molding clay
- Natural gas
- Salt
- Sandstone

FISHING

- Commercial
  fishing

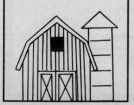

OHIO

SPORTS AND RECREATION

Water sports are available on Ohio's numerous lakes.
Skiing and winter sports are popular near Akron.
Golf, horseback riding, hiking, and camping are
available. The Cincinnati Reds baseball team
and the Cincinnati Bengals football
team play at Riverfront Stadium.
The Cleveland Indians' home is
Municipal Stadium.

ATTRACTIONS OF INTEREST

☞ Pro-Football Hall of Fame—Canton

☞ "Tecumseh," historical outdoor drama—
Chillicothe

☞ Cincinnati Zoo and Botanical Garden

☞ Cincinnati Fire Museum

☞ Museum of Natural History—Cincinnati

☞ Graron Woods Village—Sharonville

☞ B.B. Riverboat Cruise—Cincinnati

ECONOMY

- ⇨ Natural gas
- ⇨ Research in plastics, aviation, glass, rubber, and chemicals
- ⇨ Steel production
- ⇨ Soap
- ⇨ Oil

1ST FAMOUS FIRSTS

Nation's first coeducational college—Oberlin College, 1833

Rubber manufacturing center—Goodrich made rubber products in Akron

Inventions—cash register, electric runabout, and automobile self-starter

FAMOUS PEOPLE

Neil Armstrong

Clarence Darrow

Clark Gable

James Garfield

John Glenn

Ulysses S. Grant

Rutherford B. Hayes

FURTHER INFORMATION

Chamber of Commerce
35 E. Gay ST
Columbus, OH 43215

OKLAHOMA

**46th State,
November 16, 1907**

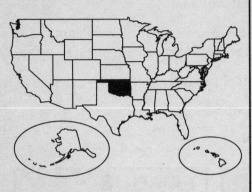

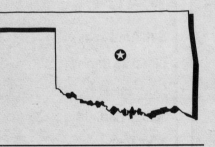

★ **QUICK FACTS** ★

CAPITAL: Oklahoma City

POPULATION: 3,174,775

AREA: 69,919 sq mi,
ranks 18th

NICKNAME: Sooner State

MOTTO: "Labor Conquers
All Things"

BIRD: Scissor-tailed
flycatcher

TREE: Redbud

FLOWER: Mistletoe

SONG: "Oklahoma!"

TIME ZONE: Central, DST

HIGHEST POINT: 4,973 ft,
Black Mesa

LOWEST POINT: 287 ft,
Little River

POSTAL ABBREVIATION: OK

GEOGRAPHY

Oklahoma is a prairie state with many mountains. It is a
southern central state bordering Colorado on the north,
Missouri and Arkansas on the east, Texas and New
Mexico on the south and west. The Arkansas River
McClellan-Kerr Waterway connects Oklahoma to the Gulf
of Mexico by way of the Mississippi River.

148

HISTORY

Oklahoma comes from two Choctaw Indian words meaning "red people." Francisco Vásquez de Coronado in 1541 explored Oklahoma for Spain. With the Louisiana Purchase in 1803, the United States got most of Oklahoma from France. The western panhandle region became a U.S. territory in 1845. In 1890, this region was divided into Indian territory and Oklahoma territory. In 1907, the two were joined to make the state of Oklahoma. The first homesteading was permitted in 1889. Those who beat the gun that started the race for homesteads at noon, April 22, 1889, were called "Sooners," the origin of the state's nickname.

AGRICULTURE	MINING	FISHING
• Wheat	• Helium	• Catfish
• Sorghum	• Iodine	• Bass
• Hay	• Coal	• Sunfish
• Cotton	• Clay	• Perch
• Peanuts	• Gypsum	• Crappie
• Mung beans	• Zinc	• Trout
• Corn	• Cement	
• Alfalfa	• Copper	
• Cattle		
• Dairy products		
• Broiler chickens		
• Sheep		

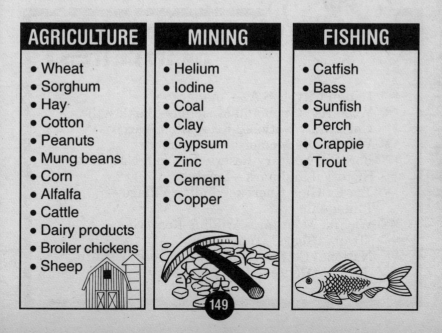

149

OKLAHOMA

SPORTS AND RECREATION

Water sports can be enjoyed at the many freshwater lakes, ponds, and reservoirs. Ouachita, Arbuckle, and Wichita Mountain areas offer many outdoor recreational activities. State parks have caverns and caves to explore, sand dunes, canyons, and mountain climbing. Spectator sports include University of Oklahoma Sooners and Oklahoma State Cowboys of college football.

ATTRACTIONS OF INTEREST

- ☞ Indian City, U.S.A.—Anadarko
- ☞ Woolaroc Ranch and Museum—Bartlesville
- ☞ Chickasaw National Recreation Area
- ☞ Will Rogers Memorial—Claremore
- ☞ Fort Sill Military Reservation and National Historic Landmark—Lawton
- ☞ Tsa-La-Gi, a Cherokee Indian Village—Tahlequah
- ☞ Wichita Mountains Wildlife Reserve
- ☞ "Trail of Tears"–Tahlequah
- ☞ National Cowboy Hall of Fame and Western Heritage Center—Oklahoma City

ECONOMY

⇨ Natural gas

⇨ Manufacturing: oil equipment, carpeting, plastics, mobile homes, transportation equipment, wood and paper products, machinery, food products, and glass

FAMOUS FIRSTS

First settlement—Miller Court House and Three Forks
First producing oil well—1889
First in Indian population

FAMOUS PEOPLE

Woody Guthrie

General Patrick Harley

Mickey Mantle

Oral Roberts

Will Rogers

Jim Thorpe

FURTHER INFORMATION

Oklahoma Tourism & Recreation Dept.
500 Will Rogers Bldg.
Oklahoma City, OK
73105–4492

OREGON

**33rd State,
February 14, 1859**

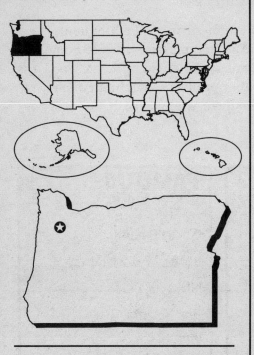

CAPITAL: Salem

POPULATION: 2,921,921

AREA: 97,073 sq mi

NICKNAME: Beaver State

MOTTO: "She Flies with Her Own Wings"

BIRD: Western meadowlark

TREE: Douglas fir

FLOWER: Oregon grape

SONG: "Oregon, My Oregon"

TIME ZONE: Pacific, DST

HIGHEST POINT: 11,239 ft, Mt. Hood

LOWEST POINT: Sea level, Pacific Ocean

POSTAL ABBREVIATION: OR

GEOGRAPHY

The Pacific Ocean is to Oregon's west, Washington State to its north, Nevada and California to its south, and Idaho to its east.

HISTORY

Oregon is called the Beaver State because of the beaver skins sold during fur-trading days. Many Indian tribes were the first to live in Oregon. Then parts of Oregon were claimed by Spain, England, Russia, and finally the United States. John Astor, an American fur trader, began the American settlement of Oregon and became known as the Father of Oregon. After the Civil War, many people moved west to Oregon. During World War II, many factories manufactured military equipment.

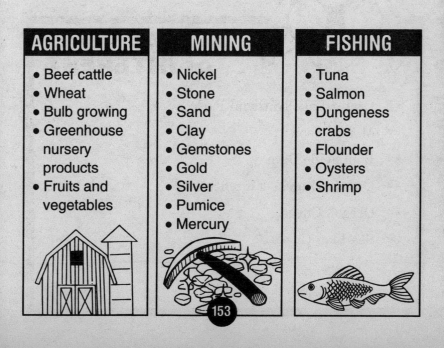

AGRICULTURE

- Beef cattle
- Wheat
- Bulb growing
- Greenhouse nursery products
- Fruits and vegetables

MINING

- Nickel
- Stone
- Sand
- Clay
- Gemstones
- Gold
- Silver
- Pumice
- Mercury

FISHING

- Tuna
- Salmon
- Dungeness crabs
- Flounder
- Oysters
- Shrimp

OREGON

SPORTS AND RECREATION

Its vast coastline, dams, and lakes offer many water sports. Sand dunes are popular for dune buggy riding. Carnivals, rodeos, festivals, skiing, and winter sports are available at different times of the year.

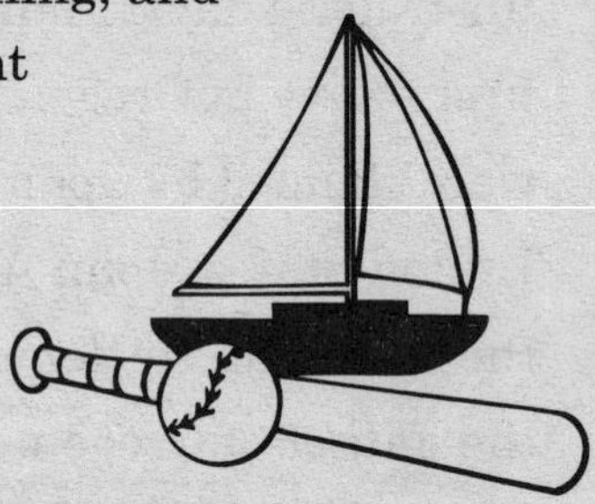

ATTRACTIONS OF INTEREST

☞ Crater Lake National Park

☞ Mount Hood

☞ Bonneville Dam

☞ Oregon Dunes—Florence

☞ Oregon Caves

☞ Sea Lion Caves

ECONOMY

⇨ Wood

⇨ Tourism

⇨ Farm, mineral, and wood products

1ST FAMOUS FIRSTS

The first U.S. government in the Pacific Northwest was organized in 1843 by Oregon settlers in Willamette Valley.

In 1902, Oregon made it possible for voters to take part in the making of laws, which became known as the Oregon System.

FAMOUS PEOPLE

John Astor

Captain Robert Gray

Mark Hatfield

James Polk

George Vancouver

Marcus Whitman

FURTHER INFORMATION

Travel Information Section
Oregon Dept. of Transportation
101 Transportation Bldg.
Salem, OR 97310

PENNSYLVANIA

**2nd State,
December 12, 1787**

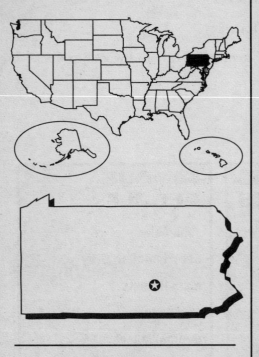

GEOGRAPHY

A mid-Atlantic state, Pennsylvania is bordered on the south by the Mason-Dixon Line, on the east by the Delaware River, on the west by West Virginia and Ohio, and on the north and northeast by Lake Erie and New York.

PENNSYLVANIA

HISTORY

Pennsylvania was named to honor Admiral Sir William Penn, the father of William Penn who came to the New World in 1862 looking for religious freedom. It means "Penn's woodland." Penn made friends with the natives and paid them for their land. The Declaration of Independence was signed in 1776 in Philadelphia, the seat of government from 1776 to 1800. Also in Philadelphia the U.S. Constitution was written in 1787. The Liberty Bell is in Philadelphia.

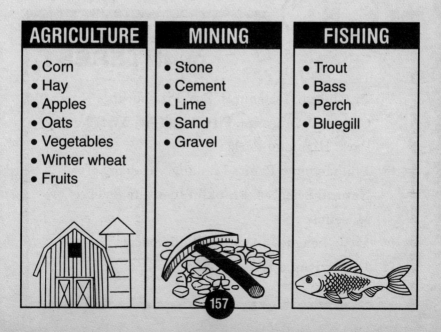

AGRICULTURE

- Corn
- Hay
- Apples
- Oats
- Vegetables
- Winter wheat
- Fruits

MINING

- Stone
- Cement
- Lime
- Sand
- Gravel

FISHING

- Trout
- Bass
- Perch
- Bluegill

PENNSYLVANIA

SPORTS AND RECREATION

The mountains and cities offer biking, tennis, golf, hiking, and cross-country skiing trails, as well as swimming pools and horseback riding. Spectator sports include Pittsburgh Steelers football, Philadelphia Eagles football, Philadelphia Phillies baseball, Pittsburgh Pirates baseball, Philadelphia 76'ers basketball, Philadelphia Flyers hockey, and Pittsburgh Penguins hockey.

ATTRACTIONS OF INTEREST

☞ Pittsburgh: Pittsburgh Zoo, Pittsburgh Children's Museum, Pittsburgh Aviary, Schenley Park, Highland Park

☞ Philadelphia: Penn's Landing, Academy of Natural Sciences, Franklin Institute Science Museum

☞ Little League Museum—Williamsport

☞ Pennsylvania Dutch region

ECONOMY

- ➪ Tourism
- ➪ Agriculture
- ➪ Manufacturing: apparel, machinery, food and food products, chemicals, and steel

1ST

FAMOUS FIRSTS

First commercially successful oil well in the United States—1859

First paved road, The Pennsylvania Turnpike—1795

First Continental Congress—1763

First full-scale nuclear power reactor for electricity—1957

FAMOUS PEOPLE

James Buchanan

Andrew Carnegie

Bill Cosby

Benjamin Franklin

Andrew Mellon

Betsy Ross

FURTHER INFORMATION

Chamber of Commerce
222 N. 3rd ST
Harrisburg, PA 17101

RHODE ISLAND

**13th State,
May 29, 1790**

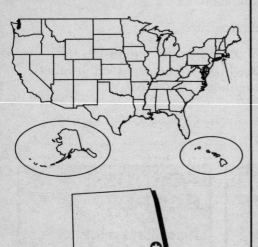

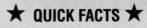

★ QUICK FACTS ★

CAPITAL: Providence

POPULATION: 1,004,328

AREA: 1,212 sq mi, ranks 50th

NICKNAME: Ocean State, Little Rhody

MOTTO: "Hope"

BIRD: Rhode Island Red

TREE: Red maple

FLOWER: Violet

SONG: "Rhode Island"

TIME ZONE: Eastern, DST

HIGHEST POINT: 812 ft, Jerimoth Hill

LOWEST POINT: Sea level, Atlantic Ocean

POSTAL ABBREVIATION: RI

GEOGRAPHY

Rhode Island lies on the Narragansett Bay. It is one of several coastal lowlands along the Atlantic Ocean.

RHODE ISLAND

HISTORY

The name Rhode Island comes from the Greek island of Rhodes. Roger Williams founded Providence. He supported freedom of religious beliefs. He had been exiled from the Massachusetts Bay Colony in 1636. The colonists defeated the Narragansett Indians in the Great Swamp Fight in 1675. Rhode Island became independant of Great Britain in May 1776. Its location on the ocean gives it its nickname: the Ocean State. Because it is so small it is also called "Little Rhody."

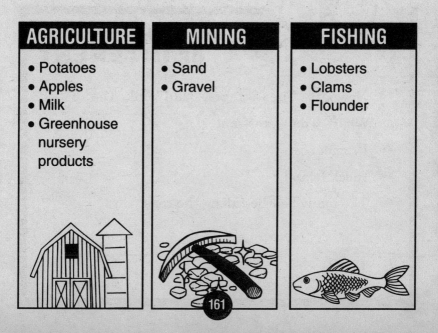

AGRICULTURE
- Potatoes
- Apples
- Milk
- Greenhouse nursery products

MINING
- Sand
- Gravel

FISHING
- Lobsters
- Clams
- Flounder

RHODE ISLAND

SPORTS AND RECREATION

It offers sailing and yacht races, jazz festivals, and many miles of beaches for swimming and hiking. Cultural events are held throughout the year. Some are held in the famous "cottages," which really are beautiful mansions. These mansions were once used as summer houses many years ago.

ATTRACTIONS OF INTEREST

☞ Newport: "The Cottages," Cliff Walk, The Wharf, The Waterfront

☞ Providence

☞ Block Island

☞ The many beaches along the coast

ECONOMY

⇨ Tourism

⇨ Manufacturing: costume jewelry, textiles, and machinery

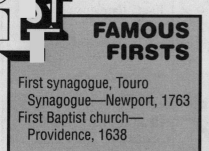

FAMOUS FIRSTS

First synagogue, Touro
    Synagogue—Newport, 1763
First Baptist church—
    Providence, 1638

FAMOUS PEOPLE

Nelson Eddy

Jabez Gorham

George Loban

Gilbert Stuart

FURTHER INFORMATION

Chamber of Commerce
30 Exchange TERR
Providence, RI 02908

SOUTH CAROLINA

**8th State,
May 23, 1788**

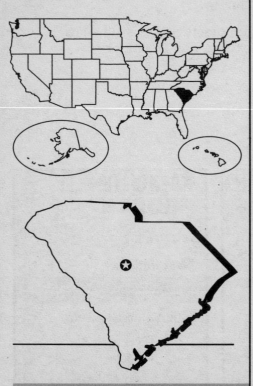

GEOGRAPHY

South Carolina is a southern Atlantic coastal state, with North Carolina to its north, the Atlantic Ocean on its east, southeast, and south, and Georgia on its southwest and western borders.

HISTORY

South Carolina was named for King
Charles I of England in 1629. In 1730,
"South" was added to the name. During the
Revolutionary War, many important battles
were fought in South Carolina. In one such battle in 1776,
while the British were trying to capture Charleston harbor,
colonists in a fort built of palmetto logs defeated a British
fleet. The British ships went up in flames; the smoke from
the flames looked like a palmetto tree, thus South
Carolina's nickname.

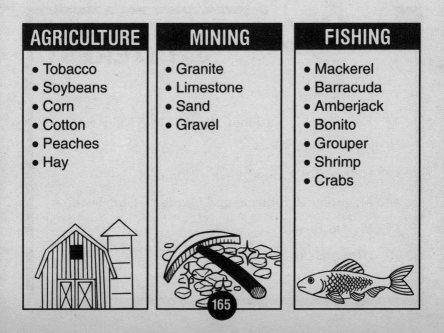

AGRICULTURE	MINING	FISHING
• Tobacco	• Granite	• Mackerel
• Soybeans	• Limestone	• Barracuda
• Corn	• Sand	• Amberjack
• Cotton	• Gravel	• Bonito
• Peaches		• Grouper
• Hay		• Shrimp
		• Crabs

SOUTH CAROLINA

SPORTS AND RECREATION

South Carolina offers an abundance of outdoor recreation. With its miles of beaches, water sports are quite popular. Golfing and tennis championships have become popular at its resorts. Shellfishing and fishing are also popular. Collegiate team sports draw many spectators.

ATTRACTIONS OF INTEREST

- ☞ Charleston
- ☞ Fort Sumter National Monument—Charleston Harbor
- ☞ Hollywolld Animal Park—Edmund
- ☞ Magnolia Plantation and Garden—Charleston
- ☞ Myrtle Beach
- ☞ Hilton Head Island

ECONOMY

⇨ Tourism

⇨ Agriculture

⇨ Manufacturing: natural and synthetic textile fibers, automobile parts, furniture, clothing, and chemicals

1ST FAMOUS FIRSTS

First state to secede from the Union before the Civil War, on December 20, 1860

First rice crops raised—1685 by H. H. Woodward from a seed given to him by a ship's captain

First fireproof building—1882

First opera performance—1702

First steam locomotive in service—1830

FAMOUS PEOPLE

John Calhoun

Jesse Jackson

James Longstreet

Thomas Sumter

Strom Thurmond

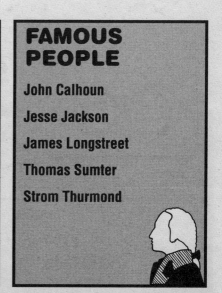

FURTHER INFORMATION

Dept. of Parks, Recreation and Tourism
Inquiry Division, Box 71
Columbia, SC 29202

SOUTH DAKOTA

**40th State,
November 2, 1889**

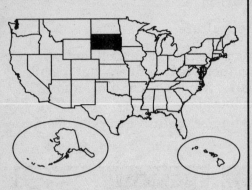

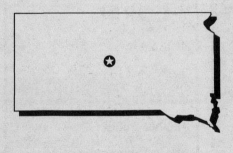

CAPITAL: Pierre

POPULATION: 703,301

AREA: 77,116 sq mi, ranks 16th

NICKNAME: Coyote State, Rushmore State

MOTTO: "Under God, the People Rule"

BIRD: Ring-necked pheasant

TREE: Black Hills spruce

FLOWER: American pasqueflower

SONG: "Hail, South Dakota"

TIME ZONE: Central/Mountain, DST

HIGHEST POINT: 7,242 ft, Harney Peak

LOWEST POINT: 962 ft, Big Stone Lake

POSTAL ABBREVIATION: SD

GEOGRAPHY

A midwestern state of the north central United States, South Dakota is bordered to its east by Minnesota and Iowa, to its south by Nebraska, to its west by Wyoming and Montana, and to its north by North Dakota.

SOUTH DAKOTA

HISTORY

The name South Dakota comes from the
Dakota tribe, meaning "allies," or
"friends." The Sioux called themselves Dakota
or Lakota. In 1874, gold was discovered on Sioux
territory and miners rushed here. The Sioux were forced to
give up their land. Indian uprisings in 1890 began again,
ending with the massacre of Indians at Wounded Knee.
The brothers, Les Verendryes, the first Europeans in the
state, introduced the fur-trading industry. The arrival of
the first steamboat on the upper Missouri in 1831
increased the fur trade.

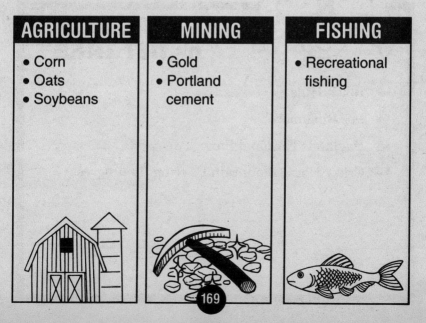

AGRICULTURE	MINING	FISHING
• Corn • Oats • Soybeans	• Gold • Portland cement	• Recreational fishing

SOUTH DAKOTA

SPORTS AND RECREATION

The rolling hills of the Great Plains and the beauty of the Black Hills offer magnificent vistas. Hiking, camping, and exploring are popular activities. The lakes offer water sports and fishing. Mountain climbing is popular in the Black Hills. Hunting is available throughout South Dakota.

ATTRACTIONS OF INTEREST

☞ Black Hills

☞ Mt. Rushmore

☞ Badlands National Park

☞ Crazy Horse Mountain Carving (in progress)

ECONOMY

- ⇨ Agriculture
- ⇨ Finance/ Banking
- ⇨ Insurance
- ⇨ Real estate
- ⇨ Tourism
- ⇨ Manufacturing: machinery, electronic and electrical equipment, and food products

1ST FAMOUS FIRSTS

First in gold production
First successful navigation of a steamboat on the upper Missouri River—the *Yellowstone*, 1831, to Fort Tecumseh
First explorers of South Dakota—Les Verendryes, 1743. They buried a lead plate at what is now Fort Pierre as proof of their visit.

FAMOUS PEOPLE

Sparky Anderson
Tom Brokaw
Calamity Jane (Martha Jane Burk)
Crazy Horse
Mary Hart
Cheryl Ladd
George McGovern
Sitting Bull

FURTHER INFORMATION

South Dakota Tourism
711 E. Wells AVE
Pierre, SD 57501–3369

TENNESSEE

**16th State,
June 1, 1796**

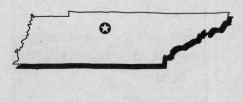

★ QUICK FACTS ★

CAPITAL: Nashville

POPULATION: 4,952,726

AREA: 42,144 sq mi,
ranks 34th

NICKNAME: Volunteer State

MOTTO: "Agriculture and
Commerce"

BIRD: Mockingbird

TREE: Tulip poplar

FLOWER: Iris

SONG: "Tennessee Waltz"

TIME ZONE:
Eastern/Central, DST

HIGHEST POINT: 6,643 ft,
Clingman's Dome

LOWEST POINT: 182 ft,
Mississippi River

POSTAL ABBREVIATION: TN

GEOGRAPHY

A southeastern central state, Tennessee's northern
borders are Kentucky and Virginia. East is North
Carolina, west are Arkansas and Missouri, and south
are Georgia and Alabama.

HISTORY

The name Tennessee comes from Tanasie, a Cherokee village in the region. Tennessee is sometimes called "Big Bend State," because of its bend in the Tennessee River. It's also called the "Volunteer State" because of its military traditions. Tennessee was first explored by the Spaniard, Hernando de Soto, in 1541, followed by English traders crossing the Great Smokies from the east, and the French on the west sailing down the Mississippi River in 1673. Virginians first settled here in 1769. Many Civil War conflicts were fought here, with over 30,000 soldiers fighting with the Union.

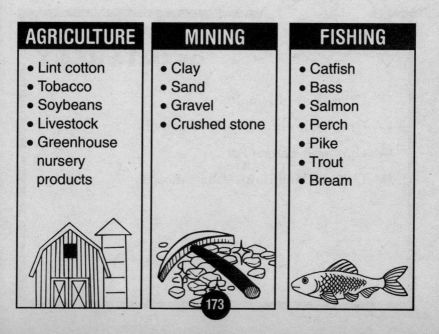

AGRICULTURE

- Lint cotton
- Tobacco
- Soybeans
- Livestock
- Greenhouse nursery products

MINING

- Clay
- Sand
- Gravel
- Crushed stone

FISHING

- Catfish
- Bass
- Salmon
- Perch
- Pike
- Trout
- Bream

TENNESSEE

SPORTS AND RECREATION

Tennessee has many mountains, lakes, and reservoirs. There are numerous water sporting opportunities. Winter sports include downhill and cross-country skiing.

ATTRACTIONS OF INTEREST

- ☞ Graceland—Memphis
- ☞ Grand Ole Opry House—Nashville
- ☞ Opryland Theme Park
- ☞ Lookout Mountain—Chattanooga

ECONOMY

⇨ Tourism

⇨ Manufacturing: machinery, electronics, and chemicals

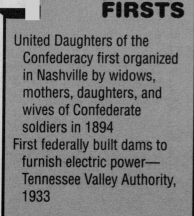

FAMOUS FIRSTS

United Daughters of the Confederacy first organized in Nashville by widows, mothers, daughters, and wives of Confederate soldiers in 1894

First federally built dams to furnish electric power— Tennessee Valley Authority, 1933

FAMOUS PEOPLE

Davy Crockett

Albert Gore

Sam Houston

Elvis Presley

Dinah Shore

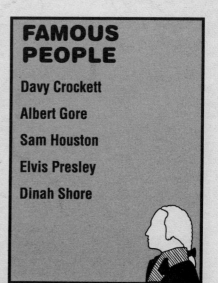

FURTHER INFORMATION

Dept. of Tourist Development
Rachel Jackson Bldg.
Fifth Floor
Nashville, TN 37219

TEXAS

**28th State,
December 29, 1845**

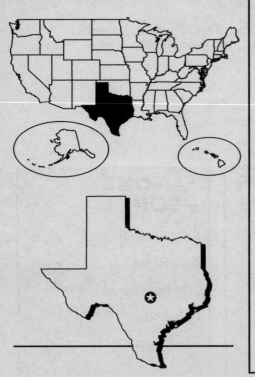

★ QUICK FACTS ★

CAPITAL: Austin

POPULATION: 17,348,206

AREA: 266,807 sq mi, ranks 2nd

NICKNAME: Lone Star State

MOTTO: "Friendship"

BIRD: Mockingbird

TREE: Pecan

FLOWER: Bluebonnet

SONG: "Texas, Our Texas"

TIME ZONE: Central, DST

HIGHEST POINT: 8,751 ft, Guadeloupe Point

LOWEST POINT: Sea level, Gulf of Mexico

POSTAL ABBREVIATION: TX

GEOGRAPHY

Texas is a southwestern state. The Gulf of Mexico is to its southeast; its southwest borders Mexico, separated by the Rio Grande. Oklahoma, Alabama, Louisiana, and New Mexico also border Texas.

HISTORY

The name Texas comes from the Indian word *tejas*, which means "friends" or "allies." The Tejas were a group of united Indian tribes. Texas, originally owned by Spain, was part of Mexico when the first Americans arrived in the early nineteenth century. Texas's struggle for independence began in 1835. In 1836, the president of Mexico, General Antonio López de Santa Anna, and his army staged a siege at the Alamo, overcoming about 185 defenders. Sam Houston's Texans later defeated Santa Anna at San Jacinto. Texas became a state in 1845. Six nations have ruled Texas: Spain, France, Mexico, the Republic of Texas, the Confederate States of America, and the United States.

AGRICULTURE

- Cotton
- Grain
- Vegetables
- Peanuts
- Livestock

MINING

- Cement
- Stone
- Sand
- Gravel

FISHING

- Commercial fishing

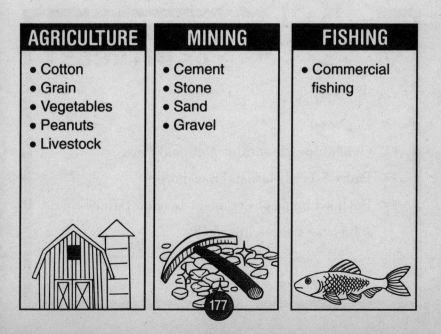

SPORTS AND RECREATION

Horseback riding, hiking, tennis, golf, and water sports are all offered in Texas. Popular among Texans is the variety of sports offered, such as the Dallas Cowboys, Houston Oilers, and the Cotton Bowl in football. The National Basketball Association's teams are the Houston Rockets, the San Antonio Spurs, and the Dallas Mavericks. The Texas Rangers play baseball at Arlington Stadium. Rodeos are held most weekends.

ATTRACTIONS OF INTEREST

- ☞ The Alamo
- ☞ Big Bend
- ☞ Guadalupe Mountains National Park
- ☞ Padre Island National Seashore
- ☞ Boyhood home of President Lyndon Baines Johnson—near Johnson City

ECONOMY

⇨ Trade

⇨ Services

⇨ Manufacturing: machinery, transportation equipment, electrical and electronic equipment, and clothing

1ST

FAMOUS FIRSTS

First in mineral production
First in oil refining and natural gas production
First in farming acreage
First in production of cattle, sheep, and wool

FAMOUS PEOPLE

Stephen Austin

James Baker

Carol Burnett

Howard Hughes

Lyndon B. Johnson

Mary Martin

Dan Rather

Sam Rayburn

FURTHER INFORMATION

Chamber of Commerce
900 Congress, Suite 501
Austin, TX 78701

UTAH

**45th State,
January 4, 1896**

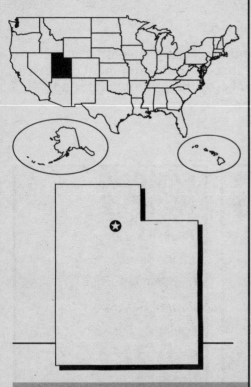

★ QUICK FACTS ★

CAPITAL: Salt Lake City

POPULATION: 1,770,212

AREA: 84,899 sq mi, ranks 12th

NICKNAME: Beehive State

MOTTO: "Industry"

BIRD: Sea gull

TREE: Blue spruce

FLOWER: Sego lily

SONG: "Utah, We Love Thee"

TIME ZONE: Mountain, DST

HIGHEST POINT: 13,528 ft, Kings Peak

LOWEST POINT: 2,200 ft, Beaver Wash Dam

POSTAL ABBREVIATION: UT

GEOGRAPHY

Utah is a western mountain state. To its south is Arizona, west is Nevada, north is Idaho, northeast is Wyoming, east is Colorado, and southeast is New Mexico.

HISTORY

The name Utah comes from the Ute tribe and means "people of the mountains." When Mormon pioneers led by Brigham Young settled this region, they called it "Deseret," the Mormon word for honeybee, meaning industry and hard work. The United States acquired Utah in 1848 after the Mexican War. Brigham Young became the governor, and the Mormons wanted to join the Union. Because they practiced polygamy, they were refused. In 1895, the Mormons outlawed polygamy and joined the Union in 1896.

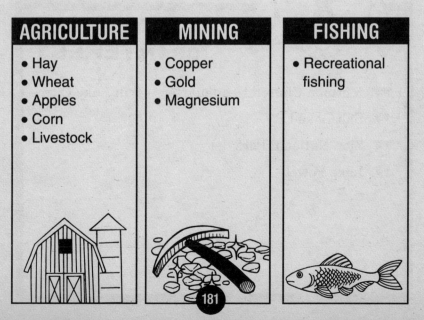

AGRICULTURE	MINING	FISHING
• Hay • Wheat • Apples • Corn • Livestock	• Copper • Gold • Magnesium	• Recreational fishing

UTAH

SPORTS AND RECREATION

Water sports are abundant on Utah's lakes and rivers. Ski resorts offer winter sports. The five national parks and six national forests are popular areas for hiking, camping, boating, fishing, and beautiful scenery for viewing.

ATTRACTIONS OF INTEREST

☞ Mormon Church Headquarters—Salt Lake City

☞ Salt Lake City

☞ Zion National Park

☞ Lake Powell

ECONOMY

➩ Services

➩ Trade

➩ Government

➩ Construction

➩ Manufacturing: guided missiles and parts, steel, and electrical equipment

1ST FAMOUS FIRSTS

First U.S. transcontinental railroad system, linking Central and Union Pacific Railroads—Promontory, 1869

First sugar beet crop—1850's; Lehi Plant (1890) started this industry

First transcontinental telegraph service—Telegraph lines met at Salt Lake City, 1861

FAMOUS PEOPLE

Maude Adams

Ezra Taft Benson

John M. Browning

David M. Kennedy

Osmond Family

Brigham Young

Loretta Young

FURTHER INFORMATION

Utah Travel Council
Council Hall, Capital Hill
Salt Lake City, UT 84114

VERMONT

**14th State,
March 4, 1791**

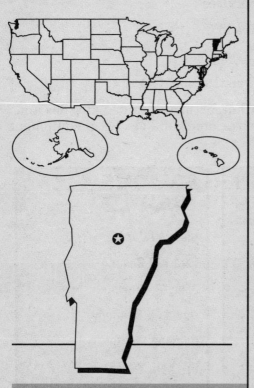

★ QUICK FACTS ★

CAPITAL: Montpelier

POPULATION: 566,619

AREA: 9,614 sq mi, ranks 43rd

NICKNAME: Green Mountain State

MOTTO: "Freedom and Unity"

BIRD: Hermit thrush

TREE: Sugar maple

FLOWER: Red clover

SONG: "Hail, Vermont!"

TIME ZONE: Eastern, DST

HIGHEST POINT: 4,393 ft, Mt. Mansfield

LOWEST POINT: 95 ft, Lake Champlain

POSTAL ABBREVIATION: VT

GEOGRAPHY

Vermont is the only New England state without a coastline on the Atlantic Ocean. The Connecticut River is its eastern border. Lake Champlain borders its northwest. In addition to the Green Mountains, Vermont has many other mountains and hills.

HISTORY

The word Vermont comes from *vert mont*, French for "green mountain." After the Revolutionary War, Vermont remained an independent republic for about ten years. On March 4, 1791, Vermont entered the Union as the fourteenth state, the first to be admitted under the Constitution. Montpelier became the capital in 1805. Prior to its entry into the Union, Vermont was an independent republic. It coined its own money, ran its own postal service, and was self-governing.

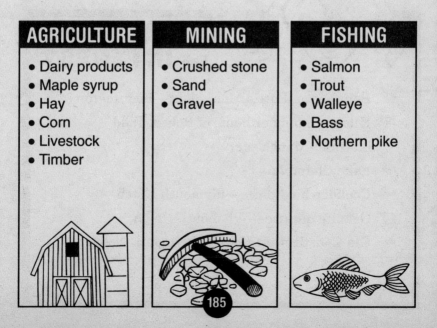

AGRICULTURE
- Dairy products
- Maple syrup
- Hay
- Corn
- Livestock
- Timber

MINING
- Crushed stone
- Sand
- Gravel

FISHING
- Salmon
- Trout
- Walleye
- Bass
- Northern pike

VERMONT

SPORTS AND RECREATION

Both summer and winter resort areas are abundant. Vermont's Green Mountains offer ideal winter sports, skiing being the most popular. The lakes offer all water sports. With 70 percent of the state covered by forests, fall foliage attracts thousands of tourists.

ATTRACTIONS OF INTEREST

☞ Bennington Battle Monument—Bennington

☞ Hildene, summer home of Robert Todd Lincoln—Manchester

☞ Lake Champlain

☞ Coolidge birthplace—Plymouth Notch

☞ Granite quarries—Plymouth Notch

☞ Old Constitution House—Plymouth Notch

ECONOMY

- ➪ Tourism
- ➪ Manufacturing: machine tools, furniture, fishing rods, books, scales, and paper

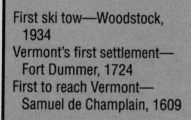

FAMOUS FIRSTS

First ski tow—Woodstock, 1934

Vermont's first settlement— Fort Dummer, 1724

First to reach Vermont— Samuel de Champlain, 1609

FAMOUS PEOPLE

Chester Arthur

Calvin Coolidge

Admiral George Dewey

John Dewey

Stephen Douglas

FURTHER INFORMATION

Vermont Dept. of
Travel and Tourism
134 State ST
Montpelier, VT 05602

VIRGINIA

**10th State,
June 25, 1788**

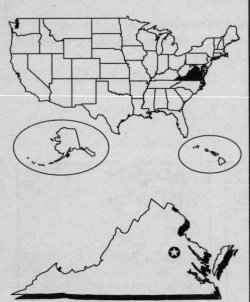

★ **QUICK FACTS** ★

CAPITAL: Richmond

POPULATION: 6,285,931

AREA: 40,767 sq mi, ranks 36th

NICKNAME: Old Dominion, Mother of Presidents

MOTTO: "Thus Always to Tyrants"

BIRD: Cardinal

TREE: Flowering dogwood

FLOWER: American dogwood

SONG: "Carry Me Back to Old Virginia"

TIME ZONE: Eastern, DST

HIGHEST POINT: 5,729 ft, Mt. Rogers

LOWEST POINT: Sea level, Atlantic Ocean

POSTAL ABBREVIATION: VA

GEOGRAPHY

Virginia has five main land regions: (1) the Appalachian Plateau, (2) the Appalachian Ridge, (3) the Blue Ridge, (4) the Piedmont, and (5) the Atlantic Coast. Ohio and Kentucky are to its west. Tennessee is to its southwest, and North Carolina is to its south. Washington, DC, and Maryland border its east and northeast.

HISTORY

The name Virginia comes from "Virgin Queen of England," in honor of Elizabeth I. Its nickname Old Dominion comes from this colony's loyalties to King Charles II during the English Civil War in the mid-1600's. Eight U.S. Presidents were born here, giving the state its other nickname, "Mother of Presidents." Virginia is one of the most historic of all fifty states, and some of the most important events of American history took place here. It was founded in 1607. During the American Revolution, Benedict Arnold burned Richmond and St. Petersburg for the British in 1781. General Charles Cornwallis, trapped at Yorktown, surrendered on October 19, 1781.

AGRICULTURE

- Tobacco
- Peanuts
- Winter wheat
- Sweet potatoes

MINING

- Crushed stone

FISHING

- Commercial fishing

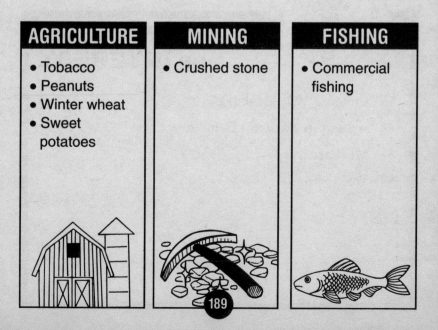

VIRGINIA

SPORTS AND RECREATION

Virginia's miles of oceanfront beaches offer resorts with opportunities for a variety of water sports. Winter sports are also popular.

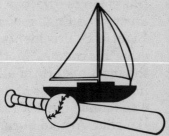

ATTRACTIONS OF INTEREST

☞ Colonial Williamsburg

☞ Arlington National Cemetery

☞ Mt. Vernon

☞ Yorktown

ECONOMY

- ➪ Service
- ➪ Trade
- ➪ Government
- ➪ Manufacturing: tobacco, chemicals, textiles, transportation equipment, rubber, and plastic products

FAMOUS FIRSTS

First permanent English settlement in America—Jamestown, 1607

Declaration of Independence written by Thomas Jefferson in 1776

First President of the United States—George Washington

First public school integration—Arlington County and Norfolk, 1959

FAMOUS PEOPLE

William Henry Harrison

Patrick Henry

Thomas Jefferson

Robert E. Lee

James Madison

James Monroe

Zachary Taylor

John Tyler

George Washington

FURTHER INFORMATION

Chamber of Commerce
9 S. Fifth ST
Richmond, VA 23219

WASHINGTON

**42nd State,
November 11, 1889**

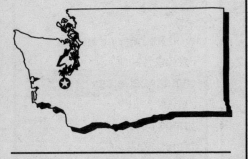

★ QUICK FACTS ★

CAPITAL: Olympia

POPULATION: 5,017,724

AREA: 68,139 sq mi, ranks 20th

NICKNAME: Chinook State, Evergreen State

MOTTO: "Alki" (Indian word meaning "By and by")

BIRD: Willow goldfinch

TREE: Western hemlock

FLOWER: Rhododendron

SONG: "Washington, My Home"

TIME ZONE: Pacific, DST

HIGHEST POINT: 14,410 ft, Mt. Rainier

LOWEST POINT: Sea level, Pacific Ocean

POSTAL ABBREVIATION: WA

GEOGRAPHY

A northwestern coastal state, Washington's eastern border is Idaho, its northern border is Canada, and its southern border is Oregon. The Pacific Ocean is to its west.

HISTORY

Washington is the only state named for a President of the United States, George Washington. Its nickname, Evergreen State, comes from its many hemlocks, firs, pines, and other evergreen trees. It was first settled by the Spanish, followed by an American, Captain Robert Gray, and then Canadian fur traders. John Jacob Astor in 1811 established a post at Fort Okanogan. In 1846, Britain and Canada established their borders. In 1855, gold was discovered, bringing new settlers.

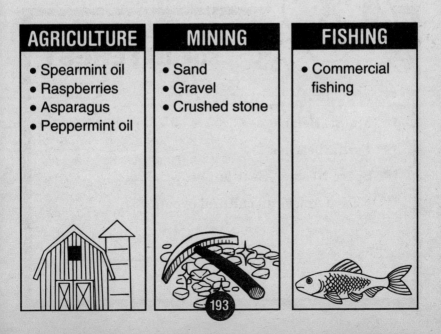

AGRICULTURE

- Spearmint oil
- Raspberries
- Asparagus
- Peppermint oil

MINING

- Sand
- Gravel
- Crushed stone

FISHING

- Commercial fishing

193

WASHINGTON

SPORTS AND RECREATION

State parks, lakes, riverfalls, 157 miles of coastline, canyons, and mountain ranges offer year-round outdoor activities such as hiking, water sports, biking, tennis, and winter sports.

ATTRACTIONS OF INTEREST

☞ Mt. Rainier

☞ Mt. St. Helens

☞ Pacific beaches

☞ Space Needle—Seattle

☞ Native American cultural events

ECONOMY

➪ Tourism

➪ Agriculture

➪ Fishing

➪ Aerospace

➪ Manufacturing: lumber, plywood, aluminum, processed fruit and vegetables, pulp, and aircraft

1ST

FAMOUS FIRSTS

First sawmill run by water power, 1826
First steam sawmill, 1853
First in lumber production

FAMOUS PEOPLE

Bing Crosby

William O. Douglas

Henry Jackson

Minoru Yamasaki

? FURTHER INFORMATION

Local Chamber of Commerce
P.O. Box 658
Olympia, WA 98507

WEST VIRGINIA

**35th State,
June 20, 1863**

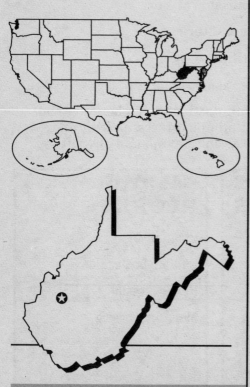

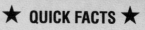

★ **QUICK FACTS** ★

CAPITAL: Charleston

POPULATION: 1,800,936

AREA: 24,087 sq mi, ranks 41st

NICKNAME: Mountain State

MOTTO: "Mountaineers Are Always Free"

BIRD: Cardinal

TREE: Sugar maple

FLOWER: Rhododendron

SONGS: "This Is My West Virginia," "West Virginia, My Home Sweet Home," and "The West Virginia Hills"

TIME ZONE: Eastern, DST

HIGHEST POINT: 4,863 ft, Spruce Knob

LOWEST POINT: 240 ft, Potomac River

POSTAL ABBREVIATION: WV

GEOGRAPHY

West Virginia is an eastern state bordered on its south and east by Virginia, by Kentucky and Ohio on its west, and Pennsylvania, Ohio, and Maryland on its north.

WEST VIRGINIA

HISTORY

Originally part of Virginia, West Virginia gets its nickname Mountain State from its mountains, steep hills, and narrow valleys. The earliest Indians were the Mound Builders, followed by Cherokee, Delaware Conoy, Shawnee, and Susquehanna. In 1776, the people of western Virginia petitioned the Continental Congress for a separate government. In 1863, West Virginia became a separate state.

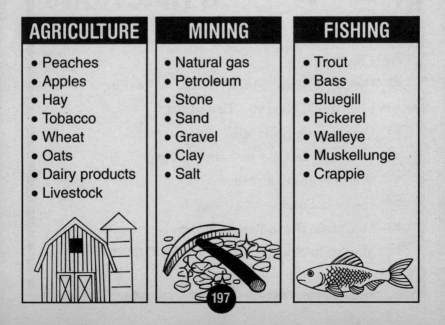

AGRICULTURE

- Peaches
- Apples
- Hay
- Tobacco
- Wheat
- Oats
- Dairy products
- Livestock

MINING

- Natural gas
- Petroleum
- Stone
- Sand
- Gravel
- Clay
- Salt

FISHING

- Trout
- Bass
- Bluegill
- Pickerel
- Walleye
- Muskellunge
- Crappie

WEST VIRGINIA

SPORTS AND RECREATION

West Virginia's rivers offer water sports; especially popular is white-water rafting. Resorts, state forests, and state parks have numerous recreational facilities enjoyed by all in winter as well as in the warmer months.

ATTRACTIONS OF INTEREST

- ☞ Charleston
- ☞ Oglebays' Good Children Zoo—Wheeling
- ☞ Lost World Cavern—Lewisburg
- ☞ Cass Scenic Railroad
- ☞ Smoke Hole Caverns—Petersburg
- ☞ White Sulphur Springs
- ☞ Harpers Ferry
- ☞ Mountain State Forest Festival
- ☞ Mountain State Arts and Crafts Fair

ECONOMY

⇨ Tourism

⇨ Mining

⇨ Services

⇨ Agriculture

⇨ Manufacturing: plastic and hardwood products, machinery, fabricated metals, organic and inorganic chemicals, steel, and glass

FAMOUS FIRSTS

First natural gas well—1815, Charleston, James Wilson

First rural free delivery—1896, mail routes from Charleston, Halltown, and Uvilla

First battle of the Revolutionary War—Battle at Point Pleasant, 1774

FAMOUS PEOPLE

Pearl S. Buck

Thomas J. "Stonewall" Jackson

Don Knotts

Nick Nolte

Cyrus Vance

Colonel Chuck Yeager

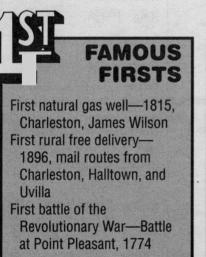

FURTHER INFORMATION

Dept. of Commerce
State Capitol
Charleston, WV 25305

WISCONSIN

**30th State,
May 29, 1848**

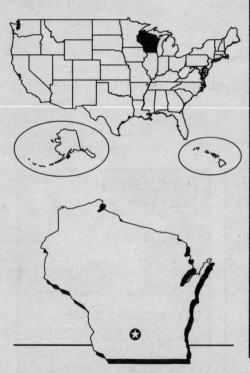

★ QUICK FACTS ★

CAPITAL: Madison

POPULATION: 4,955,127

AREA: 56,153 sq mi,
ranks 25th

NICKNAME: Badger State

MOTTO: "Forward"

BIRD: Robin

TREE: Sugar maple

FLOWER: Wood violet

SONG: "On, Wisconsin!"

TIME ZONE: Central, DST

HIGHEST POINT: 1,952 ft,
Tim's Hill

LOWEST POINT: 581 ft,
Lake Michigan

POSTAL ABBREVIATION: WI

GEOGRAPHY

A northern central state, Wisconsin's eastern border
is Lake Michigan. To the west are the St. Croix and
Mississippi Rivers, to the north, Lake Superior and
Upper Michigan.

HISTORY

The name Wisconsin has several Indian meanings—"homeland," "wild rice country," and "gathering of the waters." The nickname Badger State was first used to describe the lead miners of the 1820's, who burrowed holes in the caves dug out of the hillside. The Winnebago, Dakota, and Menominee Indians first lived in Wisconsin. Many Indians moved here in the 1600's. It belonged to France until England took it after the French and Indian War. After the Revolutionary War, in 1783, the United States took over this region, and it was part of the territories of Indiana, Illinois, and Michigan in the 1800's.

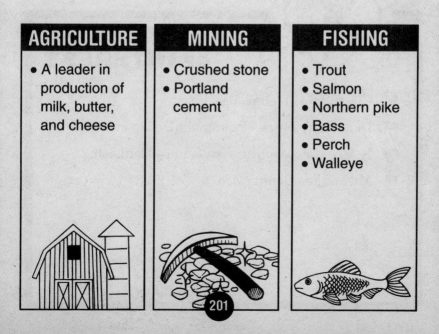

AGRICULTURE

- A leader in production of milk, butter, and cheese

MINING

- Crushed stone
- Portland cement

FISHING

- Trout
- Salmon
- Northern pike
- Bass
- Perch
- Walleye

WISCONSIN

SPORTS AND RECREATION

Wisconsin's lakes offer water sports during the summer. Many parks have hiking trails, pools, golf courses, and beaches. There are many events beginning in January. Winter sports include skiing—cross-country and downhill—snowmobiling, ice hockey, and skating. Rugby, baseball, football, hockey, soccer, and basketball all have professional teams in Wisconsin.

ATTRACTIONS OF INTEREST

☞ Circus World—Baraboo

☞ Dells Boat Tours—Wisconsin Dells

☞ E.A.A. Air Adventure Museum—Oshkosh

☞ Milwaukee County Zoo

ECONOMY

- ⇨ Tourism
- ⇨ Trade
- ⇨ Transportation
- ⇨ Government
- ⇨ Communication
- ⇨ Agriculture

- ⇨ Manufacturing: transportation equipment, wood and paper products, foods, fabricated metals, and beer

FAMOUS FIRSTS

First circus—Ringling Brothers "Big Top," 1884
First kindergarten—Margartha Schurz, 1856
First hydroelectric plant, 1882
First state to adopt the number system for marking highways
First state to adopt minimum-wage laws, 1913
First typewriter—Carlos Glidden, 1867

FAMOUS PEOPLE

Harry Houdini

Spencer Tracy

Orson Welles

Thornton Wilder

Frank Lloyd Wright

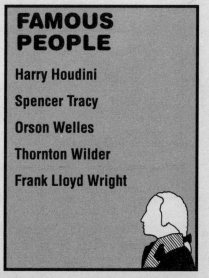

FURTHER INFORMATION

Wisconsin Dept. of Development
Division of Tourism
123 W. Washington AVE
Madison, WI 53702

WYOMING

**44th State,
July 10, 1890**

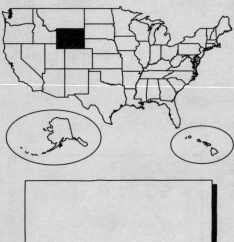

GEOGRAPHY

Wyoming is a mountain state in the Great Plains. Montana is on its northern border, Idaho on its western border, Utah and Colorado on its southern border, and South Dakota and Nebraska on its eastern border.

HISTORY

The name Wyoming comes from the Delaware Indian word meaning "upon the great plain." It is nicknamed the Equality State because Wyoming was the first state to allow women to vote, hold public office, and serve on juries. The Yellowstone area was discovered by John Colter in 1807–1808. Wyoming became a U.S. territory as part of the Louisiana Purchase. The Oregon Trail crossed Wyoming in 1812. In 1846, with the Oregon Treaty, western Wyoming was acquired by the United States. The Mexican War then ended in 1848.

AGRICULTURE

- Sugar beets
- Wheat
- Beans
- Barley
- Hay
- Livestock

MINING

- Petroleum
- Natural gas
- Coal
- Soda ash
- Sulphur
- Uranium

FISHING

- Trout
- Grapling
- Whitefish
- Bass
- Crappie
- Bluegill
- Pike

WYOMING

SPORTS AND RECREATION

Flaming Gorge National Recreation Area is a ninety-one-mile-long reservoir offering a variety of water sports. Rodeos, numerous craft exhibits, camping, mountain climbing, dude ranches, skiing, ice fishing, and amusement parks are abundant throughout the state.

ATTRACTIONS OF INTEREST

☞ Yellowstone National Park

☞ Jackson Hole

☞ Grand Teton National Park

☞ White-water rafting—Cody

☞ Cheyenne

ECONOMY

⇨ Tourism

⇨ Agriculture

⇨ Mining

⇨ Manufacturing: wood, petroleum, foods, glass, ore, lead, coal, and soda ash

1ST

FAMOUS FIRSTS

First state to give women the vote

First state to allow women to hold public office

First state to allow women to serve on public juries

First woman governor—Mrs. Millie Taylor Ross, 1924

FAMOUS PEOPLE

John Cotter

Millie Taylor Ross

FURTHER INFORMATION

Travel Commission
Etchepare Circle
Cheyenne, WY 82002